Changing Dimensions of Libraries in the Digital Age

Parveen Kumar
Librarian
I. B. College, Panipat

ATLANTIC
PUBLISHERS & DISTRIBUTORS (P) LTD

Published by
ATLANTIC
PUBLISHERS & DISTRIBUTORS (P) LTD
7/22, Ansari Road, Darya Ganj, New Delhi-110002
Phones : +91-11-40775252, 23273880, 23275880, 23280451
Fax : +91-11-23285873
Web : www.atlanticbooks.com
E-mail : orders@atlanticbooks.com

Branch Office
5, Nallathambi Street, Wallajah Road, Chennai-600002
Phones : +91-44-64611085, 32413319
E-mail : chennai@atlanticbooks.com

Printed in India at Nice Printing Press, A-33/3A, Site-IV,
Industrial Area, Sahibabad, Ghaziabad, U.P.

Preface

In a modern and dynamic library environment, digital resources has long been surpassed quantity of print resources. This paradigm shift was possible due to changing dimensions of libraries in the digital age. Although, libraries have put extra efforts to assimilate fast changes in ICT applications and are quite successful in digitizing resources to provide online information and knowledge based services. New technology has confronted librarians and information professionals with a huge challenge to survive and thrive in this digital age, where user community can access online information resources at any time and from where ever they are. Therefore, all types of libraries and information centres need to be marketed more than ever before. Libraries and information centres are known for providing valued information to users for variant purposes. Now-a-days, they can't survive without technologies, therefore they are very much using latest technologies into their services in connection to enhance the services in manifold formats. These technologies include Cloud Computing, E-Resources, Institutional Repository, Library Security, Information and Communication Technology, etc.

For clarity and understanding of the changing dimensions of libraries in the digital age, the book, containing twenty-four chapters, has been divided into six parts. First part explores the cloud computing in libraries. Cloud computing technology came up as a boon for libraries and is offering various opportunities for libraries to connect their services with clouds.

The second part is based exclusively on the concept of e-resources. Here, an effort has been made to know how e-resources are growing as a phenomenon and a very strong tool for futuristic education. The various issues relating to e-resources are discussed in this part in detail, including their uses in higher education and their overall benefits. An overview of e-resources is presented in this section. Various issues and challenges including the future of these technologies have been dealt at a length by various scholars.

The third part focuses on the concept of ICT. Effectiveness of a library service largely depends upon the Information and Communication Technology (ICT). The old functions of LIS have changed with the improvements in ICT. Librarians are expected to be higher system thinkers with proficiency to work in digital and computer communication environments.

Institutional repository has been the area of core concern for the fourth part. Institutional repository is an urgent and prompt requirement, and needs a detailed elaboration in the modern era. And the present section deals with it in a simple and lucid way.

The fifth part encompasses the chapters related to "Library Security". This part focuses on the techniques of library security in various academic libraries. The library security undoubtedly enhances the status of libraries but it lacks the applicability part in most of the institutions. The scholars are unanimous on the issue that library security must be applied in academic libraries.

The last segment (sixth part) of the book comprises the miscellaneous topics relevant to the main theme of the book. These include Modern Libraries and Learning Resource Centres: Empowering Scholars; PG College Librarians in the 21st century: Changing Roles and Responsibilities; Maintenance of Public Relations in Academic Libraries; and Sustainability Practices for Green Library as Future Transformation of Libraries.

In the accomplishment of this work I have received help from a number of individuals. I am indebted to them. Dr. (Mrs.) Ashu Shokeen, Professor, DLIS, KUK, deserves the special thanks for her continuous encouragement to complete this work. I am also thankful to Dr. J.N. Gautam, Professor, SOS in LIS, JU, Gwalior, for his valuable guidance. A special thanks to Dr. D.V. Singh, Librarian, University of Delhi, who gave valuable suggestions. I am also thankful to Dr. Suresh Dhanda, who has gone through all of the papers of my work and gave valuable suggestions. I am also grateful to all the contributors of this edited volume.

I cannot go ahead without putting into words, my deepest thanks from the inner core of my heart, for the moral support and encouragement of my beloved wife, Renu Sharma, who tried her best in providing whatever I needed, including happy and healthy family atmosphere all the time. The cherry faces of my daughter "Akshita" and my son "Anuraag" boosted me up every time to work with a new and high spirit.

With deep sense of gratitude and grateful appreciation, I just cannot limit the depth of love and indebtedness to my respected and loving parents Sh. Sat Narain and Smt. Geeta Devi, who endured forbearance in my anxious moments and sprayed their love, affection, and blessings.

Last but not least, my thanks are due to M/s Atlantic Publishers & Distributors (P) Ltd. for their untiring effort in bringing out this book well in time.

Parveen Kumar

EDITORIAL ADVISORY BOARD

Contents

Part V: Library Security

Part VI: Miscellaneous

List of Contributors

Dinesh Kumari, Librarian, BPSITTR, BPSMV, Khanpur Kalan, Sonipat (Haryana).

Rajiv Vij, Assistant Librarian, Ch. Devi Lal University, Sirsa (Haryana).

Sandhya Rani, Research Scholar, Department of Library & Information Science, Punjabi University, Patiala (Punjab).

Sapan M. Shah, Research Scholar, Library & Information Science, Veer Narmad South Gujarat University, Surat (Gujarat).

N. Bhaskara Rao, Documentation Officer, Indira Gandhi Memorial Library, University of Hyderabad, Hyderabad (Andhra Pradesh).

Gautam Soni, Assistant Librarian, Dr. Bhagwandas Central Library, Mahatma Gandhi Kashi Vidyapeeth, Varanasi (Uttar Pradesh).

Simerjit Kaur, Librarian, D.A.V. College, Pundri, Kaithal (Haryana).

Vijay Kumar Bharati, Senior Assistant Librarian, Dr. Bhagwandas Central Library, Mahatma Gandhi Kashi Vidyapeeth, Varanasi (Uttar Pradesh).

Abdul Jalil, Librarian (Associate Professor Grade), Rupahi College, Nagaon (Assam).

Ompal Singh, Senior Librarian, Government PG College for Women, Karnal (Haryana).

Sandhya Aggarwal, Librarian, M.M. College, Fatehabad (Haryana).

Vaishali M. Choudhari, Librarian, Lal Bahadur Shastri Senior College, Partur, Jalna (Maharashtra).

Devendra Kumar Sharma, Professor, Dept. of LIS, Madhav University, Abu Road (Rajasthan).

Krishna Kumar Kesharwani, Assistant Librarian/Assistant Professor Library Science, Central Library, Dr. B.R. Ambedkar University, Agra (Uttar Pradesh).

Jai Prakash Singh, Assistant Librarian/Assistant Professor Library Science, Central Library, Dr. B.R. Ambedkar University, Agra (Uttar Pradesh).

D.B. Shinde, Librarian, Arts & Commerce College, Ashta, Sangli (Maharashtra).

Vyas Jagdish R., Librarian, D.G. Tatkare Arts & Commerce College, Tala (Maharashtra).

S.N. Chobe, Librarian, K.K.M. College Manwat, Parbhani (Maharashtra).

Harmanpreet Singh Sandhu, Librarian, DAV Institute of Engineering and Technology, Jalandhar (Punjab).

Madan Lal Jat, Assistant Librarian, Kanya Gurukul Campus Haridwar, Gurukul Kangri Vishwavidyalaya, Haridwar (Uttar Pradesh).

R. Pommal Rao, Assistant Librarian (Senior Scale), Indira Gandhi Memorial Library, University of Hyderabad (Andhra Pradesh).

Narender Kumar, Assistant Librarian, Dr. Bhim Rao Ambedkar Library, Guru Jambheshwar University of Science and Technology, Hisar (Haryana).

P.C. Meena, Librarian, S.S. Jain Subodh P.G. College, Jaipur (Rajasthan).

P. Srinivasulu, Assistant Librarian, Indira Gandhi Memorial Library, University of Hyderabad (Andhra Pradesh).

Umesh Sharma, Librarian, Maharaja Ganga Singh University, Bikaner (Rajasthan).

Prashant Goswami, Assistant Library Information Officer, National Institute of Industrial Engineering, Mumbai (Maharashtra).

Part I
CLOUD COMPUTING

1

Applications of Cloud Computing with Special Reference to Libraries

Dinesh Kumari

ABSTRACT

Cloud computing is the recently emerged approach. Its applications are used in different fields. Libraries are also facilitating cloud-based services to its user to provide services effectively. This chapter makes us familiar with cloud computing and its services, and explore Cloud computing applications for various library services.

Keywords: *Cloud; Cloud Computing; Library Services; E-resources.*

Introduction

Cloud computing is the most recent emerging and utility-oriented approach in which we store and access data by a specific type of network instead of physical device which we have. The term 'cloud' refers to a network which is present at remote, and 'Cloud Computing' refers manipulating, configuring, and accessing the applications online. Cloud computing has been adopted in many various for effective services. Cloud computing has large potential for libraries also. Libraries are providing their services through cloud platform to access these services anywhere and anytime.

Numerous definitions are used to signify the concept of cloud computing. Some of them are as under:

According to Wikipedia, "Cloud computing is internet based computing, whereby shared resources, software, and information are provided to computers and other devices on demand, like the electricity grid."

According to Gartner, "Cloud computing is a style of computing in which massively scalable IT-related capabilities are provided as a service to external customers using internet technologies."

According to Greble, "Cloud computing is a technology that uses the internet and central servers to maintain data and applications. Cloud computing allows consumers and businesses to use applications without installation and access their personal files at any computer with internet access. This technology allows for much more efficient computing by centralizing storage, memory, processing and bandwidth."

According to Pew Internet Trust, "Cloud computing is a phrase that is being used today to describe the act of storing, accessing and sharing data, applications and computing power in cyberspace."

In fact, cloud computing is a new form of computing that used virtualized infrastructure by which one can access the applications as utilities, over the Internet without worrying about any maintenance or management of actual resources.

Elements of Cloud Computing

- Software
- Hardware
- Virtual Private Networking
- Private Network

Types of Cloud

There are basically four types of clouds which are as under:

Public cloud: It provides a common storage space which is based on the concept of multi tenancy and used by public. For example, Google, Yahoo, etc.

Private cloud: It is based on private infrastructure managed by private organizations.

Community cloud: It completes the specific requirement of a community. For example, college student group, Rajasthani club, LIS community, etc.

Hybrid cloud: It is the combination of two or more different types of cloud infrastructure. It may be public-community, public-private, public-hybrid, etc. For example, Railway reservation, etc.

Cloud Computing Models

Cloud computing has three service models:

Software-as-a-Service (SaaS): It is a service model which tries to make availability of software in the cloud, e.g. Google Docs., E-Mail, etc.

Platform-as-a-Service (PaaS): It provides a platform for software development and extension of existing applications, e.g. Google App.

Infrastructure-as-a-Service (IaaS): It provides infrastructure for users to obtain and use computing resources, e.g. Amazon Web Service, HP, IBM, etc.

Need of Cloud Computing

Strategic and technical direction

Efficiency and effectiveness

Speed and agility

Performance, availability and reliability.

Characteristics of Cloud Computing

Self-healing and reduce business risk: Every application which runs in a cloud computing environment always has a hot back-up without disruption.

No up-front investment: Cloud computing gives the ability to rent services which is based on a pay-per-use principle.

Scalability and elasticity: These services are linearly scalable in which workload can be breakdown into pieces and elasticity is the ability to scale resources, both up and down, as and when required.

Service-oriented: Cloud computing allows re-use of the different services which are available and that are being created.

Easy Access: Cloud computing provides web-based services which are easy to access through any device.

Virtualization: It is a process in which the customers share the infrastructure without being aware of the sharing. It hides the computing platform's physical characteristics from users.

Resource-pooling: The system allows several customers to share the infrastructure allotted to them. It is done in a way that privacy and security of their data is not compromised.

Mobility: It has the mobility characteristics because users can access applications at any time and at any place.

Applications of Cloud Computing

Cloud computing has wide range of applications in different domains which are given as under:

- Scientific e.g. HPC, HTC
- Biological e.g. ECG
- Healthcare e.g. protein structure prediction
- Geosciences e.g. GIS
- Business and Consumer e.g. CRM, ERP
- Social networking e.g. facebook
- Media e.g. video processing operations
- Productivity e.g. Google Doc.

Applications of Cloud Computing in Libraries

Nowadays, cloud computing is being adopted as a service in the libraries to deliver the library functions in an effective manner, and various other services are being provided by the cloud. In libraries, for various services cloud computing is emerged as one of the most popular technologies. In libraries, following areas are identified where cloud computing applications can be applied:

- **To Store Data:** Storage of the library data (Bibliographic, Digital, Technical, Administrative, Licenses) is the key application in libraries. Cloud computing provides many services for file storage and access like Flicker, Jungle disk, Dropbox, Google Doc and so on.

- **To Build Digital Library and Repository:** Cloud computing is used to build digital library and repository. Some open source and other softwares are available like DSpace and Fedora Commons.
- **Core Library Services:** To provide core library services i.e. storage and dissemination, acquisition, cataloguing, process system, digital content etc. Cloud computing is using popular technology like OCLC which is offering various library core services on cloud platform through the web share management system.
- **Web-OPAC:** To provide effective library services Web-OPAC can be hosted on cloud like University of Mysore Web-OPAC.
- **Union Catalogue of Serials:** CSIR and DST labs are the examples of this cloud-based service.
- **To Host E-Library:** E-Library may also host on cloud platform like Western State College of Colorado.
- **To Browse Data/Library Metadata:** To search library data, some popular services are also available on cloud like OCLC World Cat Service.
- **Resource-Sharing:** It is also a key feature of libraries. Nowadays INFLIBNET encourages this concept by providing many web-based resources through UGC-Infonet Digital Library Consortium which is based on cloud computing platform.
- **To Share Library/Scholarly Content:** To share the library content i.e. collections, subscriptions, digital print and publishing some integrated search facility are provided on cloud platform. Knimbus is cloud-based research platform which facilitates to discover and share the scholarly content.
- **To Build Community:** Cloud computing is also helpful for libraries to build their community with the help of social network and services i.e. LIS community.
- **To Avoid Plagiarism:** Many cloud-based plagiarism services are available; for example Urkund's e-mail-based

system automatically checks all submitted documents with no extra efforts required on the part of the authority.

- **Other Applications:** Apart from these, there are some other areas also like Inter Library Loan Services, Archive management and online references, provided on cloud platform.

Advantages of Cloud Computing in Libraries

- Unlimited storage facility
- Cost-effectiveness
- Remote access
- Easy accessibility
- Round the clock availability
- Flexibility
- Integration and exchange of data
- Create and collaborate

Examples of Cloud Computing in Library/Services

- OCLC
- Library of Congress (LC)
- Mendeley
- LibLime Koha
- Cyberarian
- Scribd
- Discovery Service
- Google Docs/Google Scholar
- World Cat
- Zimbra
- Encore
- Dura Cloud
- Google-based cloud services

Challenges in Implication of Cloud Computing in Libraries

While cloud computing has many advantages for library functions, still there are some challenges in its implementation. These are listed below:

- Lack of technical skills in LIS professionals as most of the professionals are not familiar with the concept of cloud computing.
- Lack of good service providers as applications of cloud computing is higher in personal use than in library operations and services.
- Data security, Data ownership (requirement to retain control) and Data privacy (Patron records) are also main issues to provide cloud-based library services.
- Lack of adequate Internet facilities create problems like service doesn't work well with low speed connection and features might be limited or slow.
- Some other issues like lack of adequate infrastructure and budget are also some barriers in adoption of cloud-based library services.

Conclusion

In recent times, the needs of users are shifting towards a different environment, and to meet the changing needs of users, the libraries are required to adopt service systems of hybrid nature, there is a need for libraries to become of hybrid nature. Cloud computing technology is a new way and can be a great benefit to libraries in publicizing their collections and services after resolving some issues related to cloud platform. Many software vendors and third party services are offering hosting of various library services on cloud to save libraries from investing in hardware for this purpose.

In fact, in some areas, libraries are using cloud computing in successful mode, but in other areas, a fair amount of work is needed to be done so that libraries may put more and more contents into the cloud.

References

Bollavarapu, S. and Gupta, B. 2014. Data Security in Cloud Computing. *International Journal of Advanced Research in Computer Science and Software Engineering*. 4(3).

Gosavi, Nandkishore, Shinde, Seetal S. and Dhakulkar, Bhagyashree. 2012. Use of cloud computing in Library and Information Science Field. *International Journal of Digital Library Services*. 2(3), 51-60.

http://crd-aida.ro/RePEc/rdc/v2i1/14.pdf

http://www.exforsys.com/tutorials/cloud-computing/cloud-computing basiccomponents/1.html

http://www.gartner.com/technology/topics/cloud-computing.jsp

https://www.gartner.com/it/initiatives/pdf/KeyInitiativeOverview_CloudComputing.pdf

https://www.ibm.com/developerworks/community/blogs/c2028fdc-41fe-4493-8257

https://www.slideshare.net/weelibrarian/cloud-computing-for-libraries-an-introductioninflibnet.ac.in/caliber2013/ppt/2_19.pptx

Kaur, Kulveen 2013. Moving libraries to the cloud. *International Journal of Information Dissemination and Technology.* 4(1), 28-30.

Kaushik, A. and Kumar, A. 2013. Application of cloud computing in libraries. *International Journal of Information Dissemination and Technology*. 3(4), 270-73.

Raghavendra, R., Indrani, V and Narayana, Poornima. Impact of Cloud Computing Technology for Library Services. Information Centre for Aerospace Science & Technology National Aerospace Laboratories.

Sareen, P. 2013. Cloud Computing: Types, Architecture, Applications, Concerns, Virtualization and Role of IT Governance in Cloud. *International Journal of Advanced Research in Computer Science and Software Engineering*. 3(3), 533-38.

Tabbii, Y., Enjajjar, I. and Bankaddour, A. 2014. Security in Cloud Computing approaches and solutions, IEEE.

Zhang, Q., Cheng, L., and Boutaba, R. 2010. Cloud computing: State-of-the-art and research challenges. *Journal of Internet Services and Applications*. 1(1), 7-18.

2

Application of Cloud Computing in Libraries: Impact, Issues and Standards

Rajiv Vij

ABSTRACT

Cloud computing is a new technology model for Information Technology services that many businesses and organizations are adopting. Cloud computing has provided us a new perspective to look at the current resource sharing problem. It can be applied to digital library resources to improve information sharing capabilities and to improve resource utilization. But as more and more information relating individuals, organizations and companies is placed in the cloud, several concerns are arising about just how safe an environment it is. The chapter discusses how cloud computing solutions could be beneficial to libraries in three basic areas: technology, data and community. It presents clear idea about cloud computing while discussing security issues, requirements and challenges that Cloud Service Providers face during cloud engineering. Recommended security standards and management models to address these are suggested for libraries and technical of business organizations.

Keywords: *Cloud Computing; Cloud Vendors; Data Privacy; Data Protection; Virtualization.*

Introduction

Cloud computing is a new technology model for information technology and library services, which many organizations, libraries and individuals are adopting. It allows these organizations and individuals to avoid locally hosting and operating multiple servers over an organization's network and constantly dealing with hardware failure, software installation, upgrades, backup and compatibility issues and also enable them to save cost. As far as user is concerned, a cloud is a service that satisfies all of the following conditions:

- It is delivered over telecommunications network.
- Users place reliance on the service for data.
- The access of the data arises processing is under the legal control of the user.
- The user doesn't need any technical awareness about which server is running or which host is delivering the service, nor where the hosting device is located.
- The service is acquired under a relatively flexible contractual arrangement.

The phrase cloud computing means "a type of Internet-based computing," where different services—such as servers, storage and applications—are delivered to an organization's computers and devices through the Internet. Ogbu and Lawal (2013) emphasized that cloud computing offers a new dimension in computing, it changes how we invent, develop, scale, update, maintain and pay for applications and the infrastructure on which they run.

Definitions

There is potential for a lot of confusion surrounding the definition of cloud computing. According to McKinsey (2009), "Clouds are hardware-based services offering compute, network and storage capacity where: Hardware management is highly abstracted from the buyer. Buyers incur infrastructure costs as variable OPEX (operational expenditure), and infrastructure capacity is highly elastic (up or down)."

National Institute of Standards and Technology (NIST) defines cloud computing as "...is a model for enabling convenient, on-demand network access to a shared pool of configurable computing resources (for examples, networks, servers, storage, applications, and services) that can be rapidly provisioned and released with minimal management effort or service provider interaction".

According to Wikipedia, "Cloud computing is Internet-based computing, whereby shared resources, software, and information are provided to computers and other devices on demand through the Internet."

FZI (Jens Nimis): "Building on compute and storage virtualization, cloud computing provides scalable, network-centric, abstracted IT infrastructure, platforms, and applications as on-demand services that are billed by consumption."

Some more serious definitions:

Colayer (2009) defines cloud computing to "the delivery of computing as a service rather than product, whereby shared resources, software and information are provided to computers and other devices as a metered service over a network, typically the Internet".

"...means using web services for our computing needs which could include using software applications, storing data, accessing computing power, or using a platform to build applications".

The basic emphasis of these models are that organizations buy and pay for the services instead of investing in hardware and software.

Types of Cloud

Libraries may soon be building and managing their own data centres. In addition to all the hype and optimism surrounding cloud computing, there are still significant fears and doubts which organizations point out. In particular, the major cloud computing vendors haven't yet fully addressed concerns about security, privacy and reliability. However, the following types of cloud computing are available:

- **Private Cloud**—It is that type of cloud computing which is owned by an organization, individually or personally. It is an arrangement for a specific group or organization which is accessible only to that organization. In private cloud, an organization converts its facilities into cloud and then provides the services to the users. That is why, it is known as internal cloud. Example: Amazon, VPC, VMC are Cloud Infrastructure Suite, Institutional Cloud, EBay.
- **Public Cloud**—Public Cloud Service is a kind of external service. It is shared by various clients or customers. It is owned by anyone but used by others after giving charges for hiring the services just like lease service. The owner maintains its own norms, policies, procedures, values, profit system and charging criteria. Example: Race space, Amazon, Google, Microsoft Azure, IBM Smart cloud and Force.com.
- **Hybrid Cloud**—It is a combined computing model of public, private community and other models, depending on the need and requirement of user. A hybrid cloud is primarily based in a privately-owned and operated data center, but it can shift some of its traffic and data processing requests to public cloud vendors. All the clouds are sustaining their uniqueness and performing together in a group. Under this type of clouding, organizations are focusing on the requirement of the users and then providing service. Example: Google Apps, Windows Azure, VMware Vcloud (hybrid cloud services).
- **Community Cloud**—If the thought of "building and managing your own data center" sends chills down your spine, you might consider a community cloud. In this cloud, service is provided by a group of organizations to the users. Community cloud is having features like mission, objective, policies, security system and compliance consideration, etc. It may be internal or external. Example: Gmail, Google Apps, Google Apps for government, Microsoft government.

Cloud Computing Service Models and Their Applications in Libraries

There are mainly three types of cloud computing service models which are given as under:

1. **Software as a Service (SaaS):** It is popularly known as "software on demand". The applications are accessible from various client devices through a thin client interface such as a web browser (e.g., web-based email). The service provider provides licenses for an application to customers either as a service on demand or through subscription, in a "pay as-you-go". Examples are Google Apps Sales force, etc.
2. **Platform as a Service (PaaS):** PaaS applications are also referred to as on demand web-based solutions. Common solutions provided in this tier range from APIs and tools to database and business process management systems to security integration, allowing developers to build applications and run them on the infrastructure that the cloud vendor owns and maintains. PaaS is based on a metering or subscription model so that users only pay for what they use. According to Kroski (2009), "With PaaS, one can focus on innovation instead of complex infrastructure."
3. **Infrastructure as a Service (IaaS):** In this application, the basic emphasis is that the clients buy those resources as a fully outsourced service instead of purchasing servers, software, and data centre space or network equipment. The user does not manage or control the underlying cloud infrastructure but has control over operating systems, storage, deployed applications, and possibly limited control of select networking components. IaaS is priced on a pay-as-you-go model enabling clients to scale up or down the operations depending on their needs at any given time and pay only for what they use. (Fox, 2009)

Cloud computing has a lot of significance and impact on libraries. Libraries are welcoming the idea of joining cloud computing because of the immediate and future benefits accrued to them by way of flexibility, transparency, interoperability, availability everywhere through 24 × 7, connectivity, innovativeness and user centeredness creativity and collaboration. Neumann (2014) emphasized that "the impacts of cloud computing in libraries are enormous and therefore, require that the library professional should develop their managerial skills to be able to appreciate the turnaround features which it offers".

Cloud computing in libraries are cost savings. In an era of shrinking budgets, it gets harder with each passing year to justify the purchase and maintenance of servers that aren't in use almost all the time. Cloud computing offers price savings due to economies of scale and the fact that you're only paying for the resources you actually use. It increases the pressure on IT professionals to become well-rounded employees with highly-developed managerial skills. Knowing how to configure and network a server isn't just enough. System librarians have to manage complex projects and evaluate competing vendors on a variety of criteria. Holding vendors accountable is especially important when they manage a significant chunk of your online data and IT infrastructure. Therefore, as long as cloud security remains a significant concern, techies may be called upon to help write binding, enforceable contracts that hold vendors to certain standards with regards to reliability and security of their services. Furthermore, techies will likely be part of the teams that periodically audit cloud vendors and ensure they're performing up to the contracted standards. Cloud computing in libraries are cloud OPAC and cloud ILS. Over the past years, more and more ILS vendors have started offering cloud-hosted versions of their products. Cloud computing possess all characteristic features to facilitate cooperative benefits derivable from togetherness between and among libraries by creating openness to information accessibility and sharing. According to Hill (2012), "The trend in cloud computing will be more of e-something and e-everything in addition to e-mail, e-books, e-friends, e-lives, etc."

Advantages of Cloud Computing

Cloud computing assures maximum availability of data, application and infrastructure to the users. It also relieves burden of IT staff within organization, as routine jobs are being handled by service providers. Cloud computing can be financially advantageous for libraries as these pay for what they use and will spend significantly less for local IT services and software.

Cloud computing offers many possibilities that will help to reduce technology cost of installing and maintaining e-library and improve collaboration among users a good example is the universities in the country. Therefore, reducing cost is one of the major attractions to cloud computing. Another advantage of cloud computing is that it addresses resource management in profoundly better ways. Cloud computing has large potential for libraries. Libraries may put more and more content into the cloud. Using cloud computing user would be able to browse a physical shelf of books, CDs or DVDs or choose to take out an item or scan a bar code into his mobile device. All historical and rare documents would be scanned into a comprehensive, easily searchable database and would be accessible to any researcher. Many libraries already have online catalogues and share bibliographic data. More frequent online catalogues are linked to consortium that share resources.

According to Michael (2010), "One of the key pressures that push libraries to cloud solutions and prove to be an impediment to the migration is the availability of IT support services." Universities can open their technology infrastructures to businesses and industries for research advancements. The efficiencies of cloud computing can help universities keep pace with ever-growing resource requirements and energy cost. The extended reach of cloud computing enables institutions to teach students in new, different ways and help them manage projects and massive workloads; and when students enter the global workforce they will better understand the value of new technologies.

Issues and Standards in Cloud Security

In the current scenario, we tend to place a lot of data in the cloud, but what do we really know about its security and threats? An important aspect of moving everything into the cloud is to keep everything safe and secure. Fears over cloud security persist with hackers obtaining user information available online for notorious purposes.

- **Privacy:** is one of the more pressing issues, to the cloud and to the network security in general. It is one important aspect that must be of absolute assurance to the CSC.
- **Confidentiality:** is also most important aspect of security. It is essential that CSPs maintain all data of a CSC confidential from other users, as it moves between the communication channels.
- **Integrity:** means that no data should be modified when it is transferred from source to destination. Ensuring the integrity of the data (transfer, storage, and retrieval) really means that just the data is changed only in response to authorized transactions.
- **Data Protection:** a cloud has vast storage space. It stores huge amount of data and information. It is, therefore, necessary for the Cloud Service Providers to ensure that data privacy is maintained. Data isolation amongst users is important. Each CSC must have a separate address space and memory regions so that they do not access data or addresses that they should not be accessing.
- **Identity Management:** is important in authentication, authorization and access control. An identity management system controls access to data and information. Organizations tend to have their own identity management system. Cloud systems could integrate the CSC's identity management system with what they have.
- **Availability:** is lost when there is a denial of service attack launched on a service. All services provided by the cloud must be available at all times. CSCs must have regular and predictable access to their data and applications.

- **Application Security:** CSCs can design their own applications on the platform in the cloud with PaaS. These applications must be tested and verified by the CSP, before being made available for other users. Otherwise an attacker can create a malicious application, self-sign the application and put it up on the cloud for naive users to use them.
- **Compatibility:** Storage services provided by one vendor may not be compatible with those provided by another vendor. It is important for CSPs to design platforms in such a way that the applications or software built over them is portable to be run on and be stored on other cloud infrastructures.
- **Data Retention:** Ideally, there should be no data retention by the CSP after a legitimate request for destroying data comes from the CSC. Otherwise a hijacker could request for the data to be destroyed after hijacking the data and all data will be lost.
- **Data Security:** Enterprises that use cloud services must be sure that their data is protected wherever it goes. Enterprise can also press for encrypting its data and allow only authorized people to access the data.

Possible Threats for Service Providers and Service Customers

A CSP may face the threats relating to wrongful use of administrative credentials based on the services that a CSP provides. There will be an unauthorized access to cloud if an attacker manages to pose as a valid CSC. This may allow an attacker to tamper with the cloud. A CSP needs to be careful in providing administrative access to its employees. Carelessness of one such employee can lead to compromising of the CSP's administrative credentials and may allow an attacker to gain complete control of the cloud. We may also consider the threats that are faced by a CSC. Based on the CSC and type of service being used, the threats may be responsible for violating a CSC's privacy or safety. These are data exposure and access insecurity. The data of various customers is stored in single cloud. Due to this sharing of storage resources if the data of a CSC is not sufficiently protected using proper cryptographic management then it may lead to exposure of a CSC's data to other CSCs who might not be authorized to access this data. Similarly, due to the distributed and shared nature of a cloud, accessing cloud services may also pose threats to the CSCs. The distributed nature of cloud service allows remote access of the service. If the remote connection is not secure then it may leave an open gate for an attacker to sniff for the CSC's credentials. It is very much clear that in order to avoid the above issues and to reduce them to a minimum we need certain safety measures and standards.

Standards of Cloud Security

- **Information Technology Infrastructure Library (ITIL):** It is a set of best practices and guidelines that define an integrated and a process-based approach for managing information technology services.
- **Open Virtualization Format (OVF):** Open Virtualization Format (OVF) is a standard pertaining to portability concern. OVF provides the ability for an efficient, flexible and secure distribution of enterprise software over the cloud.
- **ITU Standard:** The ITU standard presents a sketch of issues pertaining to cloud computing and proposes a framework for cloud security. It discusses in detail, various security challenges and ways to reduce these security risks in cloud computing.

Capabilities of Security

The standard suggests the following cloud computing security capabilities to mitigate the security:

- **Trust model:** This model will enable proper authentication and authorization of different entities and components of the system.
- **Physical security:** This capability requires the access to the CSP premise should be granted only to authorized personnel and only to those locations that are necessary for the job function.

- **Interface security:** This capability secures those interfaces that are responsible for providing cloud services to various CSCs. Some of the currently used mechanisms are mutual authentication, digital signatures, encryption and integrity checksum.
- **Network security:** It provides security domain partition, border access control, intrusion detection and prevention.
- **Data isolation:** It refers to preventing access and visibility of one party's data to another party in the shared environment.
- **Data protection:** It ensures that data of a participant is sufficiently protected and no one except authorized people is allowed to temper with it.
- **Privacy protection:** It refers to protecting private data of the user and all the processing, that is done on this private data. This process includes collection, handling, storing and deletion of private data.
- **Security coordination:** This capability is responsible for coordinating all the different security controls among different cloud services.
- **PCI DSS:** Payment Card Industry Data Security Standard (PCI DSS) was released by PCI security standards council. PCI's main objective is to provide security guidelines for credit card usage and address CSP's and CSC's.

Conclusion

Cloud computing technology offers a new approach to produce solutions for old problems. These new technologies hold the concept of cost cutting and adopting better IT capabilities in enterprise, industries, universities as well as other tertiary institutions in the country. Libraries have the opportunities to improve their services and relevance in today's information society. Cloud computing is one avenue for this move into the future. No doubt, libraries are moving towards cloud computing technology in present time and taking advantage of cloud-based services especially, in building digital libraries, social networking and information communication with manifold flexibilities but some issues related to security, privacy, trustworthiness and legality are still not fully resolved. Therefore, it is time to think seriously before clubbing library services with cloud-based technologies to provide reliable and rapid services to their users.

References

Colayer 2009. What is PasS? http:ex.colayer.com/-cached/linkwhat is PasS/link.html (accessed on 29 Dec. 2011).

Fox, R. 2009. Libraries in a Cloud. OCLC sys. Serv. 25(3), 156-61.

Goldner, M.R. 2010. Wind of change: Libraries and cloud computing. BIBLIOTHEK Forschung und Praxis, 34(3), 270-75.

Hamilton, D. 2008. 'Cloud computing' seen as next wave for technology investors' *Financial Post*. 4, http://www.financialpost.com/money/story.html?id=562877 (accessed on 18.07.08).

Hill, S. 2012. e-mail, e-books, e-friends, e-lives: Inspiring individuals: Building information teams. *Panlibus Magazine*; Issue 23, Spring. Retrieved from http// solus.co.uk/downloads/panlibus.pdf

Jens, Nimis. 2010. Cloud Computing—Challenges and Opportunities GI-Regional Gruppee Karlsruhe.

Kroski, E. 2009. Library Cloud Atlas: A guide to cloud computing and storage. *Stacking the Technology Library Journal.*

M. 2012. Cloud computing for libraries: A SWOT analysis. 8th *Convention PLANNER-2012 Sikkim University, Gangtok*, 387-94.

McKinsey & Company. "Clearing the air on Cloud Computing". http://uptimeinstitute.org/images/stories/McKinsey_Report_Cloud_Computing/mckinsey_clearing_the%20clouds_final_04142009.ppt.pdf

Michael, A. 2010. A view of cloud computing communication of the ACM, 53 (04), 50-58.

Neumann, P.G. 2014. Inside Risks and Myths of Cloud Computing and Cloud Storage considering existing and new types of risks inherent in cloud services. Retrieved from http//www.csl.sri.com/users/neumann/cacm234.pdf

NIST 2014. "National Institute of Standards and Technology" NIST, Gaithersberg. Retrieved on 23/12/2014 from http//csrc.nist.gov/publications/nistpubs/800-145/SP800-145.pdf

Richard C., R. Ogbu, K and Lawal. *A*. 2013. Cloud Computing and Its Applications in e-Library Services: Nigeria in Focus. *International Journal of Innovation, Management and Technology*. 4(5), 476-79.

Wikipedia http://en.wikipedia.org/wiki/ Cloud computing (Accessed on 10.01.2017).

3

Cloud Computing: An Overview

Sandhya Rani

ABSTRACT

In present times, the technological development has brought about dynamic changes in every field of our life and library and information science in not any exception to it. Cloud computing is a recent technique of Information Communication Technology with the help of which, we have reduced the cost, enhanced accessibility of our resources as well as the elasticity and flexibility of this field. In the present study, the applicability of cloud computing, definition, models, components of cloud and its uses in the libraries have presented.

Keywords: *Cloud Computing; Models of Cloud Computing; Use of Cloud in Libraries.*

Introduction

We are living in the information age. Information is very essential for our day-to-day activities, and the most important resource for the same is Internet, which usually fulfills this requirement. Internet is the main resource where we can transform cloud computing, develop advanced softwares and educational materials, learn to assemble hardware resources and services to students and provide educators, in even the most impoverished or remote school districts in our states. This can be done without the need for advanced IT expertise at those locations (Ajith Singh and Hemalatha, 2012). Being information centers, libraries face mounting challenges in managing the assets of their collection and maintaining or improving service levels to patrons. For the past two decades, libraries have reached out their services to its patrons, initially offering physical forms to now adding multi-media items at an advance level through electronic media. In recent years, impact of cloud computing technology has been tremendous on the library and information centers and the developments are for all to witness.

Cloud computing growth has taken all the attention of various communities like researches, students, businessmen, consumers and government organizations. Information explosion is the main reason for emerging of cloud computing as lots of data in the size of PETA bytes are uploaded in the digital world every day, which requires huge storage and computing capabilities.

Today, libraries are dealing with a large number of resources and users, and the cloud computing technology provides variety of platforms in which users can browse a physical shelf of books, CDs or DVD or choose to access an item or scan a barcode into his mobile services (Taddi, 2017).

What is Cloud Computing?

Cloud computing was coined late in 2007 and currently, it has emerged as an interesting topic due to its abilities to offer flexible dynamic IT infrastructures, Qos guaranteed computing environments and configurable software services (Baldev Kumar and Surender Kumar, 2015).

Cloud computing offers a new dimension in computing, it changes how we invent, develop, scale, update, maintain and pay for applications and the infrastructure on which they are run (Ogbu, 2013). Cloud computing provides a way to the people to share distributed resources and services that may belongs to different organizations or sites. Cloud computing is used to share distributed resources via Internet in an open environment. It is a virtual pool of computing resources through Internet (Jagadish, 2017).

The cloud element of cloud computing can be seen as an acronym that stands for:

C – Computing resources

Lo – that is location independent-accessed via online means

U – Used as an utility and

D – on demand availability (Mahanta, 2017).

Definition of Cloud Computing

According to Wikipedia, "Cloud computing is Internet-based computing whereby shared resources, software, and information are provided to computers and other devices on demand."

Erik Mitchell (2010) defined cloud computing as "a pay for what you use" model, which is easy to replicate, service-oriented and scalable. The benefits of cloud computing are enormous as it saves time, reduces use of manpower and eliminates much of the hardware. Cloud computing offers benefits of efficiency, lower cost and ease by demonstrating the "business cloud". Mitchell showed how cloud computing has been adopted by many commercial applications.

Cloud computing comes into focus only when we think about what IT has always wanted to have a way to increase the capacity and to add different capabilities to the current setting without investing in new infrastructure, training new personnel or licensing new software (Gosavi, 2012).

Cloud Computing Service Models

- Software as a Service (SaaS)—to use provider's application over a network.
- Platform as a Service (PaaS)—to deploy customer-created application to a cloud.
- Infrastructure as a Service (IaaS)—rented processing, storage, network capacity.

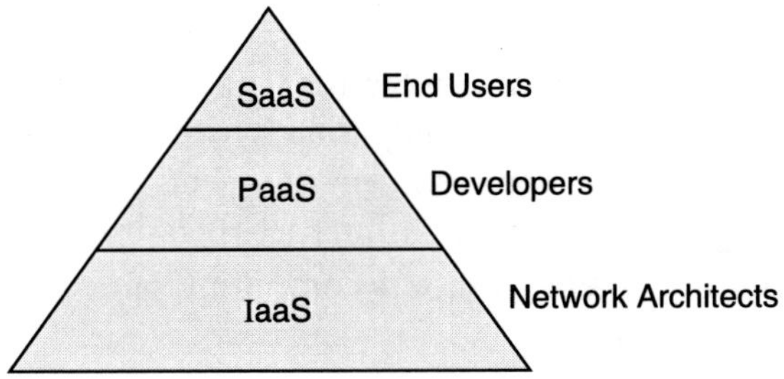

Usage of Cloud Computing in Libraries

- E-books lending service
- OPAC

- Document download service
- Current awareness service
- Bulletin board service
- Collection development
- E-learning
- Information service
- File sharing

Types of Cloud Computing

Following are the main types of cloud computing:

- **Public Cloud:** Public cloud sells service to any one on the Internet. Amazon is one of the public cloud providers. Customer has no information about the location of the cloud.
- **Private Cloud:** It is different from public cloud because it provides data to limited number of people. Private clouds are expensive but they are considered more secure than public clouds.
- **Hybrid Cloud:** This is combination of public and private computers. It has qualities of both public clouding as well as private clouding. In this type of cloud, sensitive data is stored in private cloud and other data is in public cloud.
- **Community Cloud:** Community cloud shares infrastructure between several organizations from a specific community to a common concern, whether managed internally or by a third party and either hosted internally or externally. The costs are spread over fewer users than a public cloud (but more than a private cloud), thus, only some of the cost saving potentials of cloud computing is realized.

Examples of Cloud Libraries

- OCLC
- Library of Congress
- Discovery Service

- Polaris
- Scribd
- Discovery service
- Worldcat

Advantages of Cloud Computing in Library Service

1. Quick development
2. Cost saving
3. Flexibility and innovation
4. User centric
5. Openness
6. Transparency
7. Representation
8. Interoperability
9. Availability anytime, anywhere
10. Create and collaborate
11. Easy operation
12. Outsources IT management
13. Easy maintenance and upgrade
14. User oriented
15. Connectivity and converse
16. Backup and recovery
17. Cloud environment and friendly
18. Scalability and performance

Drawbacks of Cloud Computing for Libraries

Although there are many advantages of cloud computing, there are few drawbacks of this technique, which are as under:

- Security and privacy: Libraries have a role to keep sensitive data safe, as circulation records need to be secured. Readers should also not forget that security is a major concern. For sensitive data, one must follow policies, and perform encryption to secure it in the cloud. Encryption of sensitive data and appropriate clauses in contracts which could computing service providers are good practices to keep data safe.

- Data security issues: Issues related to data security, reliability, speed, accuracy and inevitable legacy, when introducing the cloud computing services, are to be sorted out.
- Policies and procedures: Policies and procedures depend on the nature of data to be stored, size of the data and period of data to be preserved.

Conclusion

Cloud computing improves the library services in the present scenario. It can bring several benefits for librarians and give them a different future. Library and information science is moving towards cloud computing technology in present time and taking advantages of cloud-based services especially in digital libraries. Another role of LIS professionals in this virtual era is to make cloud-based services, a reliable medium to disseminate library and information services to their users with ease of use and save the time of users.

References

Ajith Singh, N. and Hemalatha, M. 2012. Cloud computing for academic environment. *International Journal of Information and Communication Technology Research,* 2(1).

Gosavi, Nandkishor, Shinde, Seetal S., and Dhakulkar, Bhagyashree. 2012. Use of Cloud Computing in Library and Information Science Field. *International Journal of Digital Library Services,* 2(3), 51-60.

Jagadish, S. 2017. Cloud Computing Use of Field in Library and Information Science. In: *Gearing Up for the Future: Library Initiatives for Digital India.* 518-26. Indian Library Association, Delhi.

Kumar, Baldev and Kumar, Surrender 2015. Cloud Computing: A Perspective Study and its Use in Educational Institution. In: *Library Automation: Issues and Remedies in Present Scenario.* 224-27. New Delhi, Manakin Press Pvt. Ltd.

Mahanta, P.K. 2017. Awareness of cloud libraries among the LIS professionals in Assam: An Analytical Study. In: *Gearing Up for the Future: Library Initiatives for Digital India.* 86-491. Indian Library Association, Delhi.

Mishan, S.A. 2013. Utilizations of Cloud Computing in Library and Information Centers: *A Theoretical Study. International Journal of Digital Library Services*, 3(4), 83-93.

Mitchell, E. 2010. Cloud computing and your library. *Journal of Web Librarianship*, 4(1).

Ogbu, Richard, C., and Lawel, A. 2013. Cloud computing and its applications in e-library services: Nigeria in focus. *International Journal of Innovation, Management and Technology,* 4(5).

Shivanand, M., and Karkun, S.G. 2017. Cloud Computing: Its Impact and Influence on Library Management and Services. In: *Gearing Up for the Future: Library Initiatives for Digital India.* 509-17. Indian Library Association, Delhi.

Taddi, Murali 2017. Cloud Computing: A New Vision. In: *Gearing Up for the Future: Library Initiatives for Digital India.* 501-26. Indian Library Association, Delhi.

Vasappagowda 2017. Application of Cloud Computing Services in Libraries: An overview. In: *Gearing Up for the Future: Library Initiatives for Digital India.* 464-76. Indian Library Association, Delhi.

Wikipedia (2017, August 6). Definition of Cloud Computing. Retrieved from http://itiinfo.om/eng.cloud-computing

4

Uses of Cloud Computing in Library

Sapan M. Shah

ABSTRACT

Cloud computing has brought a new idea to look forward to the current resource-sharing problem in digital world. This model would get library to maintain more control over the applications and data stores, in the form of sensitive and private information about patrons. Cloud computing can be applied to the digital library resources to improve information sharing capabilities and resource utilizations. This chapter explores the concept of cloud computing and its usage in the library.

Keywords: *Cloud Computing; SaaS; PaaS; IaaS; Resource Pooling.*

Introduction

Cloud computing is an emerging technology model for information technology services, which today many organizations, multinational companies and modern libraries are adopting. It allows them to avoid locally hosting multiple servers and equipments, and constantly dealing with hardware failure, software installations, upgrades and compatibility issues. For many organizations, cloud computing can simplify process and save time and money.

Cloud Computing

Cloud computing refers to applications and services that can work on a distributed network using virtualized resources and accessed by Internet protocols and networking standards of the computers. In this technology, the resources are virtual and unbounded. Cloud computing takes the technology, services and applications that are similar to those on the Internet and turns them into a self-service utility. The use of the word "cloud" makes reference to the two essential concepts which are explained as follows:

Abstraction: Cloud computing abstracts the details of system implementation from users and developers, applications, run on physical systems that aren't specified, data is stored in locations that are unknown, administration of system is outsourced to others, and access by users is everywhere.

Virtualization: Cloud computing virtualizes systems by pooling and sharing resources. Systems and storage can be provisioned as needed from a centralized infrastructure, costs are accessed on a metered basis, multi-tenancy is enabled and resources are scalable with agility.

Cloud computing can be defined as "A model for enabling ubiquitous, convenient, on-demand network access to a shared pool of configurable computing resources (e.g., networks, servers, storage, applications, and services) that can be rapidly provisioned and released with minimal management effort or service provider interaction."

Wikipedia defines cloud computing as, "Cloud computing is Internet-based computing, whereby shared resources, software, and information are provided to computers and other devices on demand through the Internet".

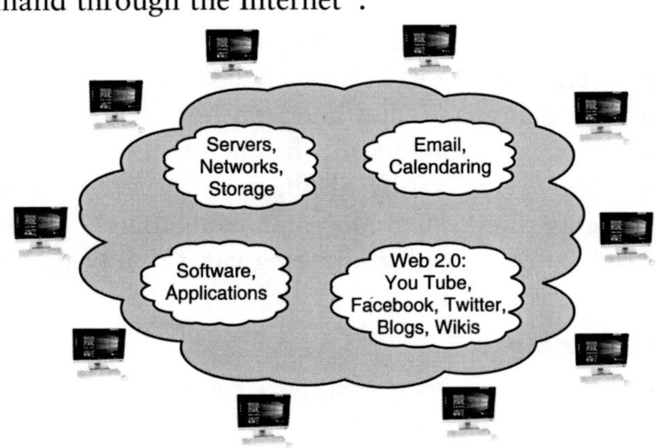

Characteristics of Cloud Computing

1. **On-demands self-service:** A consumer can unilaterally make provision for computing capabilities, such as server time and network storage, as needed automatically without requiring human interaction with each service provider.
2. **Broad network access:** Capabilities are available over the network and accessing through standard mechanisms which promote use by heterogeneous thin or thick client platforms (e.g., mobile phones, tablets, laptops, and workstations).
3. **Resource pooling:** The provider's computing resources are joined to serve multiple clients using a multi-tenant model, with different physical and virtual resources dynamically assigned and reassigned according to consumer demand. There is a sense of location independence in which the customer generally has no control or knowledge about the exact location of the provided resources but may be able to specify location at a higher level of abstraction (e.g., country, state, or data center). The basic examples of resources include storage, processing, memory, and network bandwidth.
4. **Rapid elasticity:** The capabilities can be elastically provisioned and released, in some cases automatically, to scale rapidly outward and inward commensurate with demand. For the consumer, the capabilities available for provisioning often appears to be unlimited and can be appropriated in any quantity at any time.
5. **Measured service:** Cloud systems automatically control and optimize resource use by leveraging a metering capability at some level of abstraction appropriate to the type of service (e.g., storage, processing, bandwidth, and active user accounts). Resource usage can be monitored, controlled, and reported, providing transparency to both, the provider and consumer of the utilized service.

Types of Cloud Computing

Cloud computing can be separated into following two set of models.

A. **Deployment Models:** This refers to the location and management of the cloud's infrastructure. Deployment models are of four types, viz. public, private, hybrid, and community.

(i) ***Public cloud:*** In public cloud computing services the computing resources (infrastructure) are dynamically provisioned and delivered to the user over the Internet. In this, customers have no visibility or control over where the infrastructure is located. Public cloud providers like Amazon EC2, Microsoft and Google AppEngine, Sun OCP.

Benefits of public clouds:

- Reducing the infrastructure cost.
- Allowing each individual client to operate on a low-cost, pay-as-you-go model.

(ii) ***Private cloud:*** Private cloud is cloud infrastructure dedicated to a particular organization. Private clouds allow businesses or consumers to host applications in the cloud, while addressing concerns relating to data security and control, which often lacks in a public cloud environment. It is not shared with other organizations, whether managed internally or by a third-party (e.g. institutional cloud, eBay).

Benefits of private clouds:

- Reducing TCO (Total Cost of Ownership) for operating infrastructure—hardware, power, cooling.
- Achieve a more flexible computing environment.
- Map capacity to demand.

(iii) ***Hybrid cloud:*** The cloud infrastructure is a composition of two or more separate cloud infrastructures (private, community or public) that remain unique entities, but are bound together by standardized or proprietary technology that enables data and application portability (e.g., cloud bursting for load balancing between clouds).

(iv) ***Community cloud:*** A community cloud is a multi-tenant cloud service model that is shared among several organizations and that is governed, managed, and secured commonly, by all the participating organizations or a third party-managed service provider.

Community clouds are a hybrid form of private clouds, built up and operated for a targeted group. These communities have similar cloud requirements and their ultimate goal is to work together to achieve their business objectives.

The goal of community clouds is to make participating organizations realize the benefits of a public cloud with the added level of privacy, security, and policy compliance usually associated with a private cloud. Community clouds can either on-premise or off-premise basis.

B. Service Models: This is particularly based on those type of services that any user can access on a cloud computing platform.

Software as a Service (SaaS)	• Highly scalable Internet-based applications are hosted on the cloud and offered as services to the end user. • Web-based e-Mail, Google Docs, Acrobate.com, etc.
Platform as a Service (PaaS)	• Here, the platforms used to design, develop, build and test applications are provided by the cloud infrastructure. • Google App Engine, Force.com, etc.
Infrastructure as a Service (IaaS)	• In this, pay per use models are used. Services like Storage, Database Management and compute capabilities are offered on demand. • Amazon Web Services, GoGrid, etc.

(i) *Software as a Service (SaaS):* The capability provided to the consumer is to use the provider's applications running on a cloud infrastructure platform. The applications are accessible from various client devices through either a thin client interface, such as a web browser (e.g., web-based email), or a program interface. The consumer does not manage or control over the underlying cloud infrastructure including network, servers, operating systems, storage, or even individual application capabilities, with the possible exception of limited user-specific application configuration settings.

(ii) *Platform as a Service (PaaS):* The capability provided to the consumer is to deploy onto the cloud infrastructure, consumer-created or acquired applications created using programming languages, libraries, services and tools supported by the provider. The consumer does not manage or control the underlying cloud infrastructure including network, servers, operating systems or storage but has control over the deployed applications and possibly configuration settings for the application-hosting environment.

(iii) *Infrastructure as a Service (IaaS):* The facility provided to the consumer, is to avail hardware infrastructure services for processing, storage, networks, and other fundamental computing resources where the consumer is able to deploy and run arbitrary software which can include operating systems and applications. The consumer does not manage or control the underlying cloud infrastructure but has control over operating systems, storage and deployed applications; and possibly limited control of select networking components (e.g., host firewalls).

Advantages of Cloud Computing

- To assure maximum availability of data, application, and infrastructure, one need to pay only for what has been used (i.e. Bandwidth, Resources).
- To reduce burden of IT employees within the organization, the routine jobs are being handled by service providers.
- Easily scalable as per requirement of organization.
- Another benefit of cloud computing is that it addresses resource management in profoundly, better ways. Through a cloud computing environment users can save the time and eliminate cost in services, personnel, and IT infrastructure. The major benefit of cloud computing is reducing cost and manpower.
- Lastly, the new resources requested by a user can be delivered much faster.

Disadvantages of Cloud Computing

The main disadvantages of cloud computing are dependency upon network connectivity, security, legal issues like ownership of data, latency, etc. which needs to be carefully reviewed.

Cloud Computing and Libraries

In this digital and technological era, the libraries are improving their services, relentlessly by adopting many new information technologies. The theories of conventional libraries have been changed nowadays. Introduction of new and innovative technologies like cloud technology helps libraries in improving better library services to the library community. Libraries have been using some of cloud computing services for over a decade like online databases, large union catalogues as cloud applications, the library community can further adopt the concept of cloud computing to strengthen the power of cooperation and to build a major and complex existence on the worldwide network. Following are some examples of cloud libraries:

1. OCLC
2. Library of Congress (LC)
3. Columbia Public Library
4. Ex Libris
5. Polaris
6. Scribd
7. Discovery Service
8. Google Docs/Google Scholar
9. Worldcat
10. Encore

Conclusion

Cloud computing can change the way systems are built and services delivered. It can provide libraries with an opportunity to extend their impact. Cloud computing has become a major topic of discussion and debate for any organization which relies on technology. Cloud computing is useful as it is flexible, scalable, pay as per usage, economy of scale, cost effective and maintenance fee for hardware and software, etc. The chapter discusses how cloud computing helps in acquittal libraries from managing technology so that they can focus on collection building, improved services and innovation. Cloud computing encourages libraries and their patrons to participate in a network and community of libraries by enabling them to reuse and socialize information. The cloud computing techniques and methods applied to libraries cannot only improve the quality of services and exploitation of resources, but also can make more wide use of cloud computing to our work life.

References

Appcore. Types of Cloud Computing: Private, Public and Hybrid Clouds. Retrieved June 10, 2015, from Appcore Website: http://www.appcore.com/types-cloud-computing-private-public-hybrid-clouds/

Das, K.C. (17 April 2013). Impact of Cloud Computing on Library Services. Retrieved June 15, 2015, from Central Library KIIT University. Website: http://www.kiit.ac.in/centrallibrary/pdf/pdf_presentation/Impact_of_Cloud_Computing_on_Library_Services.pdf

Liz Eversoll Cloud Services Models (aka The Cloud Stack). Retrieved June 15, 2015, from Liz Eversoll Website: http://www.lizeversoll.com/2011/01/31/cloud-services-models-aka-the-cloud-stack/

Website: http://www.nist.gov/manuscript-publication-search.cfm?pub_id=909616

Logging as a service. Retrieved June 15, 2015, from Wikipedia: http://en.wikipedia.org/wiki?curid=41067510

Mell, Peter M. and Grance, Timothy (September 28, 2011). The NIST Definition of Cloud Computing. Retrieved June 15, 2015, from National Institute of Standards and Technology.

Patel, Yatrick (2011). Feature Article: Cloud Computing and Its Impact on Library Services. INFLIBNET Newsletter. 18(1). Retrieved June 15, 2015, from Website: http://www.inflibnet.ac.in/publication/newsletter/Vol. 18, No. 1(Jan-Mar2011).pdf

Trivedi, Mayank and Suthar, Vishnu (2013). Cloud Computing: A Feasible Platform for ICT Enabled Health Science Libraries in India. *International Journal of User-Driven Health Care* (*IJUDHC*), 3(2). Retrieved June 15, 2015, from Website: http://www.igi-global.com/article/cloud-computing/86369

Yang, Jie and Liu, Wanjun (2010). Cloud Computing in the Application of Digital Library. Retrieved June 15, 2015, from Website: http://www.computer.org/csdl/proceedings/icicta/2010/4077/01/4077a939-abs.html

PART II
E-RESOURCES

5

Open Access: Best Resource Tool for Academic Community

N. Bhaskara Rao

ABSTRACT

The Open Access movement started by academicians are given boost by the library professionals in another milestone that has general way to new model of education. In this information era, libraries are involved in provided open access processes and valuable information in different ways, to their users, freely without any restrictions. The chapter discussed the importance of open access system, advantages of Open Access and the different types of open access resources which are very useful for the research community.

Keywords: *Open Access; Open Access Journals; Open Access Initiative; DOAJ; Open Source Software; Open Source Digital Repository Software.*

Introduction

Information plays a central role in the society. Knowledge in general, and information in particular, has become more necessary in life. Knowledge shared through communication is called Information. Today, access to information is no longer restricted to what is physically available in a particular library. Now, it also involves a wide variety of globally distributed commercial databases for a fee, or free of charge resources such as open access journals, open access archives and open courseware, etc. Libraries are now able to provide worldwide access to a never ending supply of distributed information and knowledge in electronic form, which is constantly updated.

Many scientific research institutions, universities and corporate R&D institutes produce high quality research accompanied by innumerable scholarly communications published by national and international journals and conference proceedings. A good number of high-quality, peer-reviewed open access journals are being published by world scholars covering a wide spectrum of subjects.

The revolution in IT offers unpatrolled opportunity for an instantaneous information communication through number of services include e-mail, online database search, CD-Search. These advancement have contributed to the development of new electronic information society.

The advent of electronic communication has extended the potential role for libraries in the information society. The tremendous advances in IT, especially, in computer and telecommunication technologies have dazzled the information age. The development of online information system has made the greatest impact on knowledge where the information has been emerged as a key resource.

Internet has made possible, an easy and a free access to the worldwide electronic and digital resources by the scientists, scholars, teachers, students and others. Electronic tools facilitate and speed up the process of dissemination of knowledge beyond the limits of printed volumes of a journal. Removing access barriers to this literature will accelerate research, enrich education, make this literature as useful. Open Access (OA) remove price barriers (subscriptions, licensing fee, etc.) and permission barriers (most copyright and licensing restrictions).

Today different types of information resources are available on the Internet such as:

- E-Journals
- E-Books
- Electronic theses and dissertations
- Course materials
- Maps
- Gray-Literature

Definitions of Open Access

The literature that should be freely accessible online is that which scholars give to the world without any expectation for payment is called Open Access.

"Open Access" means its free availability on the public Internet, permitting users to read, download, distribute, print, search, or link to the full text of these articles or use them for any other lawful purpose, without financial, legal, or technical barriers.

According to Budapest Open Access Initiative (BOAI): "Its free availability on the public interest, pertaining any users to read, download, copy, distribute, print, search, or link to the full texts of these articles, crawl them for indexing, pass them as data to software, or use them for any other lawful purpose, without financial, legal, or technical barriers other than those inseparable from gaining access to the Internet itself. The only constraint on reproduction and distribution, and the only role for copyright in this domain, should be to give authors control over the integrity of their work and the right to be properly acknowledged and cited."

According to Peter Sober, "Open Access literature is digital, online, free of charge and free of most copy right and licensing restriction, removes price barriers (most copy right and licensing, pay-per-view fees) and permission barriers (most copyright and licensing restrictions)".

The PLOS (Public Library of Science) defines OA as "free available and unrestricted use".

Advantages of Open Access

OA, to some extent, provides a solution for the pricing crisis of scholarly journals. Especially, in developing countries, the escalating prices of journal subscription and the volume of content published have risen sharply than the library budget.

OA increases the visibility of their faculty and researchers to reduce their expenses for journals, and advance their mission to share knowledge.

Improved education: The scholars can have access to the latest research findings, scientific papers and other materials throughout the world. Any user can read, download, copy or print these materials.

The Government of India has mandated all government data to be made open and available on http://www.data.gov.in. Source forges (http://www.sourceforge.net) and Github (https://github.com/) are the best sources from where one can download a huge number of software (High Wire Press: http://highwire.stanford.edu/lists/freeart.dtl; First Monday:http://firsmonday.org/htbin/egowrap/bon/obj/index.php/fm/index).

The Open Access R&D Group at the INFLIBNET Centre is working for spreading the open access movement in universities and institutions of higher learning. Major open access initiatives taken-up by the Centre includes OJAS, a platform offered to faculty and researchers in universities to host their open-access journals, and three institutional repositories, namely: ShodhGanga, ShodhGangotri and IR@INFLIBNET (from http://www.inflibnet.ac.in/activities/).

Types of Open Access

1. **Open Access Journals:** Open access journals can be defined as journals that use a funding model which does not charge readers or their institutions for access. The open access journals were founded with a mission to develop a reliable platform and to provide unrestricted access to scientific literature for rapid dissemination of recent updates in various disciplines of science and technology. Readers can access without any costs, no cost and avail the facility to enrich their scientific understanding of the relevant topics. The idea is to transcend the subscription barriers that would delay the rapid dissemination of the scientific research and hinder the access of all users for the presented information.

   Some popular open access journals are:

   (i) Directory of open access journals: DOAJ is a community-curated online directory that indexes and provides access to high quality, open access and peer-reviewed journals.

   The Directory of Open Access Journals was launched in 2003 at Lund University, Sweden, with 300 open access journals and today, it contains approx. 9000 open access journals, covering all areas of science, technology, medicine, social science, and humanities.

DOAJ is a community-curated list of open access journals and aims to be the starting point for all information searches for quality, peer-reviewed open access material. To assist libraries and indexers for keeping their lists up-to-date, public a list of journals is made that have been accepted the or removed from DOAJ but it does not discuss the specific details of an application with anyone apart from the applicant. Neither it discusses individual publishers or applications with members of the public unless it believes that, by doing so, it will be making a positive contribution to the open access community.

Aims and Scope

The aim of the DOAJ is to increase the visibility and ease of use of open access scientific, and scholarly journals, thereby promoting their increased usage and impact. The DOAJ aims to be comprehensive and cover all open access scientific and scholarly journals that use a quality control system to guarantee the content. In short, the DOAJ aims to be the one-stop shop for users of open access journals.

(Taken from https://doaj.org/about dated 24 03-2017)

(ii) *OMICS International:* OMICS International, through its Open Access Initiative is committed to make genuine and reliable contributions to the scientific community. OMICS International hosts over 700+ leading-edge peer-reviewed Open Access Journals and organizes over 3000 international conferences all over the world. OMICS International journals have over 15 million readers and the fame and success of the same can

be attributed to the strong editorial board which contains over 50000 eminent personalities that ensure a rapid, quality, and quick review process. OMICS International signed an agreement with more than 1000 international societies to make healthcare information open access. OMICS international conferences make the perfect platform for global networking as it brings together renowned speakers and scientists across the globe to a most exciting and memorable scientific event filled with much enlightening interactive sessions, world-class exhibitions, and poster presentations. (Taken from https://www.omicsonline.org, dated 24-03-2017)

(iii) *Springer Open:* Springer Open, launched in June 2010, includes Springer's portfolio of 200+ peer-reviewed fully open access journals across all areas of science. In August 2012, due to the growing demand for open access and the success of its Springer Open journals, it expanded its offering to open access books. Published under the Springer Open brand users complement its established open access journal portfolio.

Springer Open journals and books are made freely and permanently available online immediately upon publication. They are subject to high-level peer review, author and production services ensuring quality and reliability of the work. Authors publishing with Springer Open retain the copyright to their work, licensing it under a Creative Commons license. To cover the cost of the publication process, all Springer Open journals and books charge an open access fee.

Publishing with Springer Open enables authors to widen their readership, comply with open access mandates, retain copyright, and benefit from Springer's trusted brand!

(Taken from http://www.springeropen.com/)

(iv) *Elsevier-Open access journal:* All articles in open access journals which are published by Elsevier have undergone peer review and upon acceptance are immediately and permanently free for everyone to read and download. At Elsevier, we are committed to providing researchers with both green and gold open access options.

Published articles:

- Are fully peer reviewed
- Are immediately free to access and download from ScienceDirect
- Permitted re-use defined by the author's choice of Creative Commons user licenses
- Published with Cross Mark® to maintain the publication record.

(Taken from https://www.elsevier.com/about/open-science/open-access/open-access-journals)

(v) *Wiley Open Access:* Wiley Open Access journals are supported by a network of authoritative journals and societies as well as internationally renowned editorial board members. All research articles published in Wiley Open Access journals are immediately freely available to read, download and share. Wiley Open Access publishes a number of online journals across biological, chemical and health sciences.

Wiley Open Access is a program of fully open access journals. All research articles published in Wiley Open Access journals are immediately freely available to read, download and share. The fully open access journals are published in collaboration with authoritative journals and societies as well as supported by internationally renowned editorial board members.

Online Open is Wiley's hybrid open access option available on over 1300 journals. Users can visit Wiley Online Library for further details including information on Wiley's compliance with funder open access mandates. Click below to watch a video about Wiley's open access options.

(Taken from http://www.wileyopenaccess.com/view/index.html)

2. **Open Education Resources:** OER is a free and open digital publications of high quality materials organized as courses that include lectures, related reading materials, snapshots of discussions, assignments, evaluations, etc. Access to these resources radically breaks down the barriers to quality education and allows everyone to access course material that is prepared and evaluated not only by subject experts but also education experts to increase the educational utility of this material. Examples include full courses, course modules, lectures, games, teaching materials and assignments. They can take the form of text, images, audio, and may even be interactive.
3. **Open Source Software:** Open Source Software refers to software distributed in source form which can be freely modified and redistributed. Users should be free to redistribute copies, either with or without modifications, and either with or without any feed or charging a fee for distribution, to anyone, anywhere. Being free to do these things, means that the developer does not have to ask or pay for permission. The license must allow modifications and derived works, and also permit them to be distributed under the same terms as the license of the original software.

Some of the Popular Open Source Library Management Software

(i) *Koha:* Koha is the first Open Source library management system, which was initially developed by Katipo Communications with Harowhenua Library Trust, New Zealand in 2000. Now, the project has grown as one of the most popular Open Source Library

management systems by large group of volunteers from various parts of the world. The Westchester Academic Libraries Director Organization (WALDO) contracted to introduce many features into Koha required for academic libraries.

(ii) *NewGenLib:* NewGenLib is an integrated library management system developed by Verus Solutions Pvt. Ltd. Domain expertise is provided by the Kesavan Institute of Information and Knowledge Management in Hyderabad, India. Open Source Software available under GNU General Public License. Functional modules are completely web based.

(iii) *CDS/ISIS for Windows:* CDS/ISIS is a software package for generalized Information Storage and Retrieval systems developed, maintained and disseminated by UNESCO. It was first released in 1985. It is particularly suited for bibliographic applications and is used for the catalogues of many small and medium-sized libraries, versions have been produced in different world languages. UNESCO makes the software available free for non-commercial purpose, though distributors are allowed to charge for their expenses.

(iv) *Evergreen:* Evergreen is an open source Integrated Library System (ILS), initially developed by the Georgia Public Library Service for Public Information Network for Electronic Services (PINES), Development began in June 2004.

(v) *OPALS:* OPALS Open-source Automated Library System is a feature-rich, cooperatively developed, web based, open source program providing Internet access to information databases and library collections, schools, academic and cooperative regional union catalog collections use OPALS.

(vi) *OpenBiblio:* OpenBiblio is an open source Integrated Library System, which was created in 2002 by Dave Stevens. It aims to provide an easy-to-use, well-documented, easy-to-install library system. The software is popular with small and rural libraries worldwide due to its simplicity, extensive language support, and good documentation.

(vii) *PMB (PhpMyBibli):* PMB (PhpMyBibli) is a fully featured Open Source Integrated Library System. The project was initiated by Librarian Francois Lemarchand in October 2002, Director of the Public Library of Agneaux; software is now maintained by PMB services.

(viii) *Invenio:* Invenio provides user/patron management, email notification, powerful search engine that combines metadata, full text and citation search in one go, Google-like syntax, personalize account, support RSS integration for any query and support multiple output formats such as HTML, XML, MARC and OAI. It can handle medium to big data repositories.

(ix) *Emilda:* Emilda is an Integrated Library System that features an OPAC, circulation and administration functions, Z39.50 capabilities, MARC compatibility.

Open Source Digital Repository Software

(i) *DSpace:* (http://www.dspace.org) was developed jointly by the MIT library and HP Labs. DSpace modestly describes itself as a ground breaking digital repository system. It captures, stores, indexes, preserves and redistributes an organization's research material formats. DSpace supports institutional repositories and electronic records management. DSpace is being used worldwide to meet many digital archiving needs.

(ii) *EPrints:* (http://www.eprints.org) is the original digital repository software developed by the University of Southampton to manage an open archive. EPrints was the Open Archives Initiative (OAI)—Complete Repository Software. It typically supports collections of pre-prints and technical reports often subject based in scope. Recently, this software is being used/implemented to manage multidisciplinary institutional archives.

(iii) Fedora: (Flexible Extensible Digital Object and Repository Architecture (http://www.fedora.info) is a digital repository system developed jointly by Cornell University Information Science and University of Virginia Library as project. The Fedora projects goal is to provide open source repository software and related services to serve as the foundation for many different types of information management system.

(iv) Greenstone: (http://www.greenstone.org) is software for building and distributing digital library collections. This software is produced by the New Zealand Digital Library Project at University of Waikato and developed and distributed in cooperation with UNESCO and the Human Info, an NGO. It has been issued as Open Source, multilingual software under the GNU General License.

References

DOAJ: https://doaj.org

Elsevier Open access journals: https://www.elsevier.com/about/open-science/open-access/open-access-journals

Gangadharaiah, G. 2012. Management of Information Products and Services in University Libraries. New Delhi, Commonwealth Publications Pvt. Ltd.

INFLIBNET Centre: http://www.inflibnet.ac.in/activities/

OMICS: International: https://www.omicsonline.org

Open Access : http://www.openaccessjournals.com/

Open Access: Unrestricted access to published research. 2002. Budapet, 93rd Indian Science Congress, pp. 13-14 (Budapest, Open Access Initiatives, 14-2-2002).

Prasad, A.R.D. 2013. Musing on future of Librarianship: Dichotomy of Content and Form. In M. Koteswara Rao, P.V. Malleswar and Smt. A. Rajani Kumari (Eds.). A National Conference on Recent Innovations, Advancements and Challenges of Technical Libraries, Vijayawada, Vignan's University.

Raja Suresh Kumar, P. 2013. Open Source Library Management Software: PROS & CONS. In M. Koteswara Rao, P.V. Malleswar and Smt. A. Rajani Kumari (Eds.) A National Conference on

Recent Innovations, Advancements and Challenges of Technical Libraries. Vijayawada, Vignan's University, pp. 63-68.

Rajeshwar Kumar, G., Niranjan, M. and Rama Krishna Rao, E. 2013. Institutional Repositories: Challenges for Digital Libraries. In M. Koteswara Rao, P. V. Malleswar and Smt. A. Rajani Kumari (Eds.). A National Conference on Recent Innovations, Advancements and Challenges of Technical Libraries. Vijayawada, Vignan's University, pp. 109-14.

Rani, Syamalamba. Open Educational Resources (OER) for Science and Technology. In M. Koteswara Rao, P.V. Malleswar and Smt. A. Rajani Kumari (Eds.). A National Conference on Recent Innovations, Advancements and Challenges of Technical Libraries. Vijayawada, Vignan's University, pp. 55-62.

Springer Open: http://www.springeropen.com/

Sudha Rani, Y. 2013. Open Access Journals: An overview. In M. Koteswara Rao, P. V. Malleswar and Smt. A. Rajani Kumari (Eds.). A National Conference on Recent Innovations, Advancements and Challenges of Technical Libraries. Vijayawada, Vignan's University, pp. 53-54.

Wiley Open Access: http://www.wileyopenaccess.com/details/content/12f25d1df44/About.html

6

Open Access, E-Resources and Library Consortium Initiatives in India: An Overview

Gautam Soni

ABSTRACT

Dissemination of e-information and e-resources to the scholastic society and community has become an important task, though information is transmitted through various media such as periodicals, serials, journals, databases, etc. In this chapter, the importance of dissemination of information through e-resources to the academic community and the steps taken for the promotion of e-journals and e-resources in India by the reputed organizations like UGC, INFLIBNET, CSIR, etc. are discussed Consortia are all about sharing resources and improving access to information. These resources are shared among libraries that have common missions, goals and clients (users) and act on those commonalties. Before this, people were sharing own library resources through inter library loan, but in this information communication technology (ICT) age, it has gained momentum even in the developing countries. When library consortiums are formed, the existing environment about users' preferences and difficulties need to be studied. Initiating such studies would enable to incorporate the findings as the major input in consortium formation.

Keywords: *Open Access; E-Resources; Library Consortia; ICT; Digitization; Digital Library; Inter Library Loan.*

Introduction

Information and communication technologies and developments in IT have brought drastic changes in the methods of library collections over a period of time. These developments have also increased the digitization of printed material, with which libraries have implemented the just-in-time approach to collection development, and dissemination of information, especially for journals. While technology progresses rapidly in library and information centres, the size and number of journals published has also increased to accommodate the volume. New journals are being created to publish work in emerging specialist branches. This is known, as 'twigging'. Libraries with financial crunch are unable to acquire all publications that their users would generally expect to have. The increased volume of available publications have also created problems for libraries trying to provide all of the resources that their users need. Digital journals thus came into existence to come across such problems. These were first piloted in the 1980s but fully operational digital journals were not available until the 1990s. Although the majority of scholarly journal publishers operating worldwide are learned societies each publishing only one journal, a relatively small number of commercial companies dominate the market by publishing thousands of journals. Indian academic libraries are no exception to this fact and moved from print format to electronic format and formed many consortia.

What is Open Access?

The landmark Budapest Open Access Initiative (BOAI) defines Open Access "...free availability on the public Internet permitting any users to read, download, copy distribute, print, search a link to the full text of these articles, crawl them for indexing, pass them as data to software or use them for any other lawful purpose without financial, legal or technical barriers other than those in separable from gaining access to the Internet itself. The only constraint on reproduction and distribution, and the only role for copyright in this domain, should be to give authors control over the integrity of their work and right to be properly acknowledged and cited."

What is E-Resources?

An E-Resource is defined as any resource which requires computer access means resources which consists of material that are computer controlled, in which informations are stored electronically, and which are also accessible through electronic systems and networks. Any electronic product that delivers a collection of data, be it text referring to full text bases, electronic journals, image collections, other multimedia products and numerical, graphical or time based, as a commercially available title that has been published with an aim to being marketed. These may be delivered on CD ROM, on tape, via Internet and so on. The e-resources of a library includes e-journals, e-books, e-theses and dissertations, e-databases both online and offline, which should be acquired by library as per its needs, infrastructure facilities, financial provision etc. Different types of e-resources in libraries are CD-ROM, e-journals, Online Database, e-books, abstracting and indexing databases, e-mail and list servers, e-reports, e-content pages, e-clippings, etc.

Types of E-Resources

The e-resources are basically divided in two major types:

1. Online e-resources, which may include:
    - e-journal (full text and bibliographic)
    - e-books
    - online Databases
    - Web sites.
2. Other electronic resources which may include:
    - CD ROM
    - Diskettes
    - Other portable computer databases.

Advantages

- **Easy Access:** Access to a specific article or journal is easier for the users. They can access the desired material within minutes, or even seconds, on their desktops, provided, equipment is available. Large collections of material can be searched and retrieved simultaneously and instantly. There is an active dissemination of information by alerting the readers at their desktops about the new articles that are accepted into the database. In other words, electronic journals allow intelligent full-text retrieval, based on past use and interests. "Virtual issues" can be generated through dynamic interaction with the users.

- **Multi-access:** A networked product can provide multiple points of access at multiple points in time (24 hours a day, seven days a week) and to multiple simultaneous users.
- **Speed:** High speed and efficiency benefits in publishing and distributing the journals electronically. Authoring and publishing systems can be integrated easily by computer-readable text. Also, electronic transmission, especially in the review process, saves valuable time. An electronic resource is lot quicker to browse or search, to extract information from, and to integrate that information into other material and to cross-search or reference between different publications.
- **Linkages:** Linkages can be enabled by hypertext and hypermedia formats among sections within an article or among articles in journals or other electronic resources. E-Mail contacts would be easier among users, publishers and suppliers. Users have more creative ways to have their information queries answered.
- **Costs:** The journals are published electronically rather than in paper, and no new costs are introduced.
- **Multimedia:** Innovative ways of presenting research results can be supported by electronic page layout. Interactive three-dimensional models, motion video and sound are a few possibilities.
- **Functionality:** E-resource will allow the user to approach the publications to analyze its content in new ways by click of the mouse on search mode.
- **Content analysis:** E-resources contain a vast amount of information, but more importantly in a mixed format mode i.e. images, video, audio and animation which could not be replicated in print.

- **Consortia mode:** E-resources can be subscribed in a consortia format too, thus, cutting down the costs but reaping the same benefits e.g. INDEST Consortia for Engineering College Libraries.
- **Interactivity:** Articles/issues/chapters can be read, commented by the readers, amended quickly and greater feedback can be given through the web.
- **Flexibility:** Resources can be evolved quickly i.e. they are not bound to any format, printer, and distribution network.

Constraints

- **Financial constraints:** The infrastructure required displaying, storing or print electronic journals are expensive. Downloading and printing each article will be a costly affair. This means a net increase in economic and ecological costs and it becomes a relatively expensive way to acquire a single copy. Many e-journals do charge subscription fees. The pricing schemes of some suppliers are very complicated and limiting, and this might hinder libraries from utilizing e-journals.
- **Social constraints:** Electronic interfaces can take a long time to master. Electronic searching, downloading and printing replace the traditional activities of physically browsing, scanning and photocopying journal articles. The intricate steps to accomplish the previously simple or habitual tasks might frustrate users. People read up to 25 to 30 percent more slowly on a computer screen than on paper.
- **Technological constraints:** Digital journals depend upon technology and equipment for storage and display. Proper infrastructure facilities are required for the access. The academic communities can be divided into "haves" and "have-nots" because of access to equipment and network. The network or connection speed can be too slow. Screen quality of graphics and photos is still primitive when compared to print. A typical screen has a resolution of 72dpi, with at most

300dpi for some expensive and special purpose screens; while the average journal is printed at approximately 1,200 dpi.

Criteria for Selection of E-Resources

The following important issues should be taken into consideration while selecting an e-resource:

- Various number of databases offered,
- Search and retrieval facilities,
- Searchable graphic interfaces (simple and advanced user interface),
- Record formats,
- Cost factor,
- Cross reference queries,
- Service and solutions in case of problem,
- Support and training services,
- Additional facilities such as current awareness services. Selective dissemination of information,
- Varied type of usage reports.

Special Features of E-Resources

E-resources have some distinct features which differentiate them from traditional resources. E-resources on the Internet are further distinct by the nature of the information available on the net itself. The features of 21st-century information and media are (Satija, 2003):

- High compact storage;
- Ease of reproduction, multiplication and manipulation and transmutation;
- Contents can be very easily detached from its media or container;
- Ease of migration of contents from one medium to another;
- Ease of transmission, communication and storage;
- Hypertext and multimedia;

- Seamless integration of print and electronic resources;
- Sophisticated and multipronged searches through keywords, free text, Boolean operators, class numbers and natural languages processing;
- Wall-less libraries leading to the vision of multimedia global virtual library (MGVL) inaugurating an era of "Death of distance"; and
- Convergence of technology, which is getting more powerful each day.

E-Resources Made Available

- American Chemical Society (ACS) http://pubs.acs.org/about_category.html
- American Institute of Physics (AIP) http://www.aip.org
- American Physical Society (APS) http://www.aps.org
- Annual Reviews http:/arjournals.annualreviews.org
- Biological Abstracts (BA) http://webspris3.silverplattter.com/cgi-bin/erl.cgi
- Cambridge University Press Journals http://journals.Cambridge.org
- Encyclopedia Britannica http://searcheb.com/
- Institute of Physics (IOP) http://www.iop.org
- JSTOR http://www.jstor.org
- Nature http://www.aip.org
- Project muse journals http://muse.jhu.edu/journals/
- Royal Society of Chemistry http://www.rsc.org/is/journals/jl.htm
- Science Online http://www.sciencemag.org/
- SciFinder Scholar http://www.aip.org
- Engineering Science Data Unit (ESDU) www.esdu.com
- Global Market Information Database (GMID) http://www.euromonitor.com/gmid/
- INSPEC on eI Village http://www.engineeringvillage2.org//

- IEEE/IEE Electronic Library Online (IEL) http://ieeexplore.ieee.org
- Indian Standards MathSciNet http://www.ams.org/mathscinet/
- Nature http://www.npg.nature.com/libraries
- Proquest Science Journals http://www.il.proquest.com/pqdaeto
- Science Direct http://www.sciencedirect.com
- Springer Link http://www.springerlink.com

Library Consortium

A library consortium is a group of libraries who partners to coordinate activities, share resources, and combine expertise. Library consortia offer significant advantages to increasingly strapped libraries. The sharing of resources, and collaboration on shared goals often enable libraries to deliver higher quality services than they would be able to deliver on their own.

List of Library Consortium in India

- Forum for Resource Sharing in Astronomy (FORSA) – 1982
- TIFR Libraries Consortium – 1999 ISI Library Consortia Deals – 1999
- STI Network for resource sharing amongst S&T libraries – 1999 DAE Consortium – 2001
- IIM Libraries Consortia – 2001
- JCCC & VIC – 2002
- CSIR E-Journal Consortium – 2002
- INDEST-AICTE Consortium – 2003
- RGUHS-Health Science Library and Information Network (HELINET) – 2003
- UGC-INFONET Digital Library Consortium – 2004
- MCIT Library Consortium – 2005
- BJ Medical Consortium – 2006
- Consortium for e-Resources in Agriculture (CeRA) – 2007

- Electronic Resources in Medicine (ERMED) – 2008
- CSIR E-Journal Consortium now The National Knowledge Resource Consortium (NKRC) – 2009
- DRDO Consortium – 2009
- DeLCON Consortium – 2009
- National Library and Information Services Infrastructure for Scholarly Content (N-List)
- E-Shodhsindhu – 2016
- ICICI Knowledge Park.

CSIR Library Consortia (Council for Scientific and Industrial Research)

E-journals Consortia: NISCAIR is the central organization for developing a "Consortium for CSIR Laboratories for accessing e-journals". The activity shall range from creation to monitoring of the access facility of scientific periodicals published by leading international institutions. To start with, initially an agreement has been signed with, e-journal publisher, M/s Elsevier Science for a period of four years for 1200 journals. Under this scheme, CSIR scientists shall be able to access these journals and download material for their respected subjects. Such access to worldwide journal resources will play a very vital role and strengthen research and development in CSIR laboratories, thus leading to knowledge generation, useful for socio-economic development of the country.

FORSA (Forum for Resource Sharing in Astronomy and Astrophysics): It was established in 1980s, due to proliferation of information. Library professionals working in the institutes where astronomy was one of the main thrust areas of research felt the need to come together and to form a forum, which can act as a springboard for sharing and exchange of information. The sheer necessity brought all like-minded astronomy librarians in the country together and first meeting was held on July 29, 1981 at Raman Research Institute, Bengaluru and informally launched forum for resource sharing in astronomy and astrophysics FORSA with a vision and mission to share resources held in each library. Since 1989, FORSA members meet every year, in conjunction with Annual Meeting of the Astronomical Society of India. A noteworthy feature of such meetings is that FORSA members interact with the astronomers in the joint session, in which developments in library and information handling activities in the field of astronomy/astrophysics are presented and comments from users are solicited to improve and expand the horizon of library services.

HELINET (Health Sciences Library & Information Network): Health Sciences Library & Information Network is hosted by Rajiv Gandhi University of Health Sciences, Bengaluru. HELINET is the first medical library consortium launched in the country with an objective of networking the libraries affiliated to the university to promote resource sharing, especially with reference to international medical journals and databases. IIM's Library Consortia (The Indian Institute of Management): IIM Library Consortia is a Digital Library network system based on Internet technology to provide the IIM community (faculty, students and staff) an online web-enabled access to the information resources available in all the IIMs without any barriers of time and distance. It will be a simple, efficient and cost effective system. The basic operating principle of this system is decentralized acquisition, decentralized processing, and centralized utilization.

INDEST (Indian National Digital Library in Engineering Sciences and Technology): The Ministry of Human Resource Development (MHRD) has set-up the "Indian National Digital Library in Engineering Sciences and Technology (INDEST) Consortium" on the recommendation made by the Expert Group appointed by the ministry under the chairmanship of Prof. N. Balakrishnan. The Ministry provides funds required for subscription to electronic resources for institutions including IISc, IITs, NITs, IIMs and a few other centrally-funded government institutions through the consortium headquarters set-up at the IIT Delhi. Besides, government or government-aided engineering colleges and technical departments in universities have joined the consortium with financial support from the AICTE. The INDEST-AICTE Consortium is the most ambitious initiative taken so far in the country. The benefit of consortia-based subscription to electronic resources is not confined to major technological institutions in the country but is also extended to all AICTE accredited and UGC affiliated institutions. Engineering colleges and institutions have already joined the consortium on their own.

UGC-Infonet (University Grants Commission): UGC-Infonet E-Journals consortium initiative was undertaken by the Indian University Grants Commission (UGC) to facilitate free access to scholarly journals and databases in all fields and disciplines by the research and academic community across the country. All universities who are under the purview of UGC have been provided UGC-Infonet connectivity and access to scholarly E-Journals and Databases. The access is based on IP range. This effort has had a noticeable impact on the research and academic community.

DAE Library Consortia (Department of Atomic Energy): To promote interaction amongst the scientists working in the research centres of the Department of Atomic Energy and the faculty from the universities and other institutions of higher learning, and to enable young students to work on programmes of national importance under the joint guidance of the faculty from universities and the scientists of DAE so as to nurture an organic linkage between the university system and research centres of DAE, the University Grants Commission and Atomic Energy Commission have joined hands. Dr. Arun Nigavekar, the then Chairman, UGC and Dr. Anil Kakodkar, the then Chairman, Atomic Energy Commission has signed a revised MoU on 10 December 2003. Earlier both the parties entered into a MoU in July 1989 with a view to make available the facilities of the Department of Atomic Energy to the students and researchers of the university system and to involve them in the design and fabrication of systems and equipment for the setting up of new research facilities. Accordingly, the University Grants Commission created an Inter-University Consortium, with its headquarters at Indore for the utilization of the facilities established by the Department of Atomic Energy. The Inter-University Consortium has over the years taken several initiatives to foster the interaction between the university system and the DAE institutions.

Conclusion

Academic libraries have really understood that consortia based subscriptions are cost effective and also avoid redundant expenses and duplicate subscriptions. UGC-INFONET and INDEST-AICTE Consortium are two major initiatives for university library users. These revolutionary steps are providing scholarly resources including peer reviewed journals, databases, abstracts, proceedings, etc. In the long run consortia approach will be much more popular in user community and that day is not so far behind when consortia approach will expand the country's information base.

References

http://crl.du.ac.in/ical09/papers/index_files/ical-85_83_195_2_RV.pdf

http://digitalcommons.unl.edu/cgi/viewcontent.cgi?article=1913&context=libphilprac

http://eprints.rclis.org/7220/1/vijayakumarjk_09.pdf

http://ir.inflibnet.ac.in/bitstream/1944/1124/1/10.pdf

http://ir.inflibnet.ac.in/bitstream/1944/1404/1/44.pdf

http://www.csir.res.in/external/heads/pressroom/RnDNewsLetters/econsortium.pdf

http://www.ijodls.in/uploads/3/6/0/3/3603729/sunil_mansur_ok_166-177_.pdf

http://www.publishingindia.com/GetBrochure.aspx?query=UERGQnJvY2h1cmVzfC8xNjI0LnBkZnwvMTYyNC5wZGY=

https://pdfs.semanticscholar.org/a3bb/4b4d1c8ddbee97f347e0627450bbe41df1d9.pdf

nopr.niscair.res.in/bitstream/123456789/14979/1/ALIS%2059(3)%20204-211.pdf

www.alibnet.org/public/bookofpaper/9.pdf

7

Open Educational Resources in Higher Education in India: Opportunities and Challenges

Simerjit Kaur

ABSTRACT

Impact of ICT on education has brought new developments in learning resources to create a knowledge society. Use of ICT has crossed the boundaries of growth in educational resources. A number of institutions and agencies are exploring new possibilities for coping up with the educational requirements of online resources. In the higher education in India, to meet the challenges of establishing new ideas and spreading teaching learning process on the high level, open educational resources are organized through digital technology. Here, the Open Educational Resources, types of OER, major initiatives in India, and the opportunities and challenges OER have been discussed.

Keywords: *Open Education; Open Educational Resources; Higher Education; India.*

Introduction

Indian Higher Education systems in terms of institutions is very large and highly diverse in courses, management and geographical terms. "There are 785 universities, 38056 colleges and 11922 stand-alone Institutions" (Singh and Prasad, 2016). India is aspiring to establish a knowledge society in the future. For this, quality education with cost effectiveness in large environment of higher education system must be provided. This led to the increase in attention towards the educational resources in global as well as Indian contexts. The access to resources is now beyond any barrier. Online resources have bridged the gap of non-availability of resources through ICT. Now, the access to educational resources has become easy and comfortable. The online resources are now open to all to provide open education through many initiatives in India to meet the requirements of education in the country. The open educational resource (OER) movement breaks down the barriers and thus, encourages to use or share contents.

Educators worldwide are developing a vast pool of educational resources on the Internet, open and free for all to use. These educators are creating a world where each and every person on earth can access and contribute to the sum of all human knowledge. They are also planting the seeds of a new pedagogy where educators and learners create, shape and evolve knowledge together, deepening their skills and understanding as they more forward (The Cape Town Declaration 2007).

What is 'Open Education'?

"Open education (often abbreviated to OE) in higher education, is an academic practice that stresses upon a philosophy of sharing freely and openly the ideas, knowledge, methods, platforms, tools, approaches and materials used in learning and teaching. Through shared improvements in resources and techniques, quality can be enhanced to a measurable degree. Open education can also be referred to as 'open educational practice' or simply 'open practice'".

Open Educational Resources

Open Educational Resources (OER) is a relatively new phenomenon. The term Open Educational Resources has been defined by UNESCO in 2002 as: "The open provision of educational resources, enabled by information and communication technologies, for consultation, use, and adaptation by a community of users for non-commercial purposes."

In its simplest form, the concept of Open Educational Resources (OER) describes any type of educational resources which have been designed for use in teaching and learning openly. As per UNESCO guidelines, "OER has emerged as a concept with great potential to support educational transformation. While it's educational value lies in the idea of using resources as an integral method of communication of curriculum in educational courses (i.e. resource-based learning), its transformative power lies in the ease with which such resources, when digitized, can be shared via the Internet. Importantly, there is only one key differentiator between an OER and any other educational resource: its licence. Thus, an OER is simply an educational resource that incorporates a licence that facilitates reuse, and potentially adaptation, without first requesting permission from the copyright holder."

Types of Open Educational Resources

1. Media-based Text/Print: Books, materials available online e.g. Saide, Visuals, Photographs CD, DVD etc. Flickr, Pixabay, Wikimedia Commons, Open Clip Art Library, Fotopedia, Audio like Free Music Archive, and Video/Audio-Visual media resources like YouTube, Vimeo, Internet Archive, Open Yale Courses, MIT, UC Berkeley, Khan Academy etc. Animation based OER available in simulation and animation format.
2. Quality based: Self-published (through blogs, social networking etc.), reviewed, peer-reviewed material.
3. Authorship-based resources: Authorship-based resources are freely available and accessible under the licensing of creative common, open authoring like wikipedia, collaborative work.
4. License-based copyright: License-based copyright protected e-books, e-journals etc., creative commons license, public domain.

Opportunities

To provide open access to reading material in education, to reduce the cost of education, and to provide quality education, all these resources are required.

According to UNESCO, the transformative educational potential of OER revolves around three-linked possibilities:

1. **Availability:** Increased availability of high quality and relevant learning materials can contribute to more productive students and educators. Because OER removes restrictions around copying resources, it can reduce the cost of accessing educational material. In many systems, royalty payments for textbooks and other educational materials constitute a significant proportion of the overall cost, while processes of procuring permission to use copyrighted material can also be very time-consuming and expensive.
2. **Adaptation:** The principle of allowing adaptation of materials provides one mechanism amongst many for constructing roles for students as active participants in educational processes, who learn best by doing and creating, not by passively reading and absorbing. Content licences that encourage activity and creation by students through re-use and adaptation of that content can make a significant contribution in creating more effective learning environments.
3. **Capacity Building:** OER has potential to build capacity by providing institutions and educator's access, at low or no cost, to the means of production to develop their competence in producing educational materials and carrying out the necessary instructional design to integrate such materials into high quality programmes of learning.

Lifelong Learning and OER

The purpose of using OER in education is of course to enhance learning, notably a kind of learning that enables the development of both individual and social capabilities for understanding and acting. It is well established that OERs are also used for informal or non-formal learning outside formal educational settings. It is sometimes argued that to acknowledge and strengthen the importance of this role of OER, the term "education" should be replaced by "learning" and a better term would be "open learning resources".

Centre for Educational Research and Innovation

Now the digital technology is going to be accepted at all levels of education to promote the use of OER. India is a developing country with large population. It is facing a challenge of increased demand for educational resources but these resources are not at the satisfactory level till date. Hence, OERs can bridge the gap.

The National Knowledge Commission (2007) has highlighted the importance of OERs in widening the access of higher education. It has stated that "National Educational Foundation with a one-time infusion of adequate funds must be established to develop a web-based repository of high quality educational resources. OERs must be created online through a collaborative process, pooling in the efforts and expertise of all major institutions of higher education. The OER repository would supply pedagogical software for various programs run through Open and Distance Education (ODE) and be available for utilization by all Open and Distance Education (ODE) institutions. An enabling legal framework that would allow unrestricted access without compromising intellectual authorship must be devised for this purpose."

Major Initiatives in India

To improve, adapt, and grow the overall knowledge capital and its availability to all Indian students in higher education system, the National Knowledge Commission (NKC) has been constituted. One of the recommendations made by NKC is to increase the amount of Open Educational Resources (OER) and Open Access (OA).

National Portal of Technology Enhanced Learning: NPTEL is a joint initiative of IITs and IISc, funded by this mission, provides e-learning through online web and video-based courses in engineering, science and humanities streams. The mission of NPTEL is to enhance the quality of engineering education in the country by providing free online courseware. Over 329 courses are complete and made available in NPTEL website. More than 990 courses in various disciplines in engineering and science are getting generated in phase-II of NPTEL. A set of five separate DVDs containing ready NPTEL course material—one each in the areas of Electrical, Civil, Computer Science, Electronics and Mechanical Engineering was distributed to the AICTE approved Engineering Colleges during the dissemination workshop for engineering colleges of NCR Region held on 8 October 2013.

Open Education Resources (OER) through ICT initiated by NIOS: The National Institute of Open Schooling (NIOS) formerly known as National Open School (NOS) was established in November 1989 as an autonomous organization in pursuance of National Policy on Education 1986 by the Ministry of Human Resource Development (MHRD), Government of India. NIOS is also providing a number of vocational, life enrichment and community-oriented courses besides general and academic courses at Secondary and Senior Secondary level. It also offers elementary level courses through its Open Basic Education Programmes (OBE). Government of India through a gazette notification vested NIOS with the authority to examine and certify learners registered with it up to pre-degree level courses.

The National Institute of Open Schooling (NIOS) has initiated Open Educational Resources (OER) specifically for vocational programmes to be offered at Secondary and Sr. Secondary (+2) levels, including stand-alone programmes, in partnership with state level institutions and organizations. These educational resources will not only be beneficial for the students pursuing their studies through Open and Distance Learning (ODL) system at school level, but will also be accessible to millions of learners interested in development of their skills in various vocations. This will also help in vocationalization of the curriculum at Secondary and Sr. Secondary levels across the Boards in the country.

Project Oscar: Open Source Courseware Animation Repository: The main goal of Project OSCAR (Open Source Courseware Animations Repository) is to build a large repository of web-based, interactive animations and simulations, referred to as learning objects (LOs), for teaching and learning concepts in science and technology. These could be useful not only for a classroom environment but also for enabling independent learning and distance education. Prepared by IIT Bombay.

A-VIEW: (Amrita Virtual Interactive e-Learning World) is an award winning indigenously built multi-modal, multimedia e-learning platform that provides an immersive e-learning experience that is almost as good as a real classroom experience developed by Amrita e-Learning Research Lab. They are a part of Amrita Vishwa Vidhyapeetham, one of the fastest growing institutions of higher learning in India and address the most pressing issue of higher education in India—the shortage of highly qualified teachers.

A-VIEW is part of Talk to a Teacher program coordinated by IIT Bombay and they are funded by the Ministry of Human Resource Development (MHRD) under the Indian Government's National Mission for Education using Information and Communication Technology (NME-ICT) along with various other projects in Virtual Labs, Haptics and Natural Language Processing. A-VIEW is now deployed at several IITs, NITs and other leading educational institutions across the nation.

Consortium for Educational Communication popularly known as CEC is one of the Inter University Centres set up by the University Grants Commission of India. It has been established with the goal of addressing the needs of Higher Education through the use of powerful medium of Television along with the appropriate use of emerging Information Communication Technology (ICT).

eGyankosh: eGyanKosh is an initiative of IGNOU, New Delhi. It is a National Digital Repository to store, index, preserve, distribute and share the digital learning resources developed by the Open and Distance Learning Institutions in the country.

e-PG Pathshala: e-PG Pathshala is an government initiative under National Mission on Education through ICT (NME-ICT) of MHRD India, has assigned work to the UGC for development of e-content in 77 subjects at postgraduate level. The content and its quality is the key component of education system.

High quality, curriculum-based, interactive content in different subjects across all the disciplines of social sciences, arts, fine arts and humanities, natural and mathematical sciences, linguistics and languages is being developed under this initiative named e-PG Pathshala.

SWAYAM is a programme initiated by Government of India and designed to achieve the three cardinal principles of Education Policy viz., access, equity and quality. The objective of this effort is to provide the best teaching learning resources to all, including the most disadvantaged. SWAYAM seeks to bridge the digital divide for students who have hitherto remained untouched by the digital revolution and have not been able to join the mainstream of the knowledge economy. SWAYAM provides: (1) video lecture, (2) specially prepared reading material that can be downloaded/ printed, (3) self-assessment tests through tests and quizzes and (4) an online discussion forum for clearing the doubts. In order to ensure best quality content are produced and delivered, seven National Coordinators have been appointed: They are NPTEL for engineering, UGC for post-graduation education, CEC for under-graduate education, NCERT and NIOS for school education, IGNOU for out of the school students and IIMB for management studies.

Agropedia: It is an online knowledge repository of agriculture related resources in India. Agropedia is a vision which seeks to address lacunae in Indian agriculture knowledge and its application, specifically the lack of content, organized information, and extension services which are serious challenges. It has developed delivery mechanisms such as vKVK and KVK-Net, which are a means to connect extension scientists and farmers, based on its web platform which hosts information on agriculture and rural livelihood. The web platform, agropedia, is unique in the agricultural domain as it is semantically organized and enabled so as to assist one in getting exactly what information or service she or he is looking for. Along with content in the library section, certified by the Indian Council of Agricultural Research (*gyan dhara*), it also allows space for interaction, knowledge co-creation (*jana gyan*) and social networking (chat, blog, forum) making the site dynamic and learning participative.

Flexi Learn Open Course Portal IGNOU: Online Education/ e-learning Portal FlexiLearn IGNOU has online platform called FlexiLearn where more than 30,000 active users have been registered in 2010-11. It facilitates informed learning wherein anyone can register and explore courses free of cost to gain knowledge and skills in a specific area of interest. Flexi-Learn provides free and easy access to IGNOU's courses. It integrates free learning resources with learning management systems for anyone who wants to learn, whatever their educational needs and experience. Website is http://www.ignouflexilearn.ac.in/

Karnataka Open Educational Resources: The Karnataka Open Educational Resources wiki is a repository of resources to support practising teachers in terms of their professional development as well as classroom processes. The wiki is built by a community of educators who will be engaged in the creation, review, curation and publishing of digital curricular resources on a continuous basis. This resource repository is embedded in the Subject Teacher Forum that has been built across high school teachers of Karnataka. It has a link of subject portals in the section of Art, English, Hindi, ICT Literacy, Mathematics, Science, Social Science.

GeoGebra: GeoGebra is a dynamic mathematics software for all levels of education that brings together geometry, algebra, spreadsheets, graphing, statistics and calculus in one easy-to-use package. GeoGebra is a rapidly expanding community of millions of users located in just about every country. GeoGebra has become the leading provider of dynamic mathematics software, supporting science, technology, engineering and mathematics (STEM) education and innovations in teaching and learning worldwide.

TESS-India is led by The Open University and Save The Children India, funded by UK Aid, it is a multilingual teacher professional development programme which aims to support India's national educational policy by enhancing the classroom practice of primary and secondary school teachers through the provision of freely available, adaptable Open Educational Resources (OER).

The OER focuses on the development of these pedagogic practices in relation to Language and Literacy, Science, Maths, and English. Each unit includes case studies, readings, reflective tasks, and—most importantly—opportunities to apply and refine these practices in the classroom. The units are complemented by authentic videos of other Indian teachers employing new practices with their own students.

Vigyan Prasar Digital Library: Vigyan Prasar Digital Library, initiated by Vigyan Prasar, Noida, developed by Department of Science & Technology, Government of India maintains a network of science clubs across the country known as VIPNET for promoting scientific attitude among the youths and school children. Its open access digital library has 131 books (72 in English, 42 in Hindi and 17 in other languages) on significant scientific works published by Vigyan Prasar.

Brihaspati: Brihaspati, an e-Learning platform is initiated by IIT, Kanpur and is supported by Ministry of Communication & Information Technology. This platform is being used since January 2003 and is benefiting over many universities and Institutes across India.

National Digital Library (NDL): The National Digital Library (NDL) is an all-digital library that will integrate all existing digitized and digital contents across institutions of the nation to provide a single-window access with e-learning facility to different groups of users ranging from primary level to higher education level and even lifelong learners of our country. It will provide educational materials in various languages, in all disciplines, in different forms of access devices and will cater to differently-abled learners as well. NDL has been initiated to benefit all kinds of users like students (of all levels), teachers, researchers, librarians, library users, professionals, differently abled users and all other lifelong learners.

Challenges

Although it is a revolution of ICT definitely that we have a concept of OER today with us, yet there are few challenges with OERs.

1. **Sustainability:** Carrying out financial planning to ensure affordability and long-term sustainability is a challenge. Being set up cost of these resources very high for any organization which is developing the OER, it becomes necessary to ensure the sustainability of the resources. Funding is a big issue. The cost of developing the open education resources, policy-making, expansions in resources, engaging users in a long run are issues related

with sustainability. National Knowledge Commission suggests, "Initially, the government can create a grant for the generation and distribution of OER material to students and teachers from all over the country. Private industry should be the second major source of funding for developing OERs on an ongoing basis since the industry stands to benefit immensely from the improved quality of education. Private industry should be offered tax credits in return for funding and developing OER content. These partnerships with private industry will help defray the costs of development of OER material."

2. **Digital Curation and Preservation of Digital Contents:** According to Wikipedia, "Digital curation is the selection, preservation, maintenance, collection and archiving of digital assets. Digital curation establishes, maintains and adds value to repositories of digital data for present and future use. This is often accomplished by archivists, librarians, scientists, historian, and scholars. Enterprises are starting to use digital curation to improve the quality of information and data within their operational and strategic processes. Successful digital curation will mitigate digital obsolescence, keeping the information accessible to users indefinitely." The use of OERs depend a large on the infrastructure. When the contents become larger it becomes necessary to preserve for the accessibility of users. The Internet Archives, National Digital library, academic libraries, and institutional repositories are the role model in curation and preservation process. But for this process, there are many issues of fund, policies, infrastructure, access are related which needs to be addressed regularly.

3. **Object Granularity and Format Diversity:** Digital objects are made up of various sizes. Many times one object contains many sub objects. So granularity may differ. Moreover, there is format diversity in representation and coding of objects. This causes interoperability problems.

4. **Intellectual Property Issues:** The majority of existing educational contents are protected under traditional copyright agreement. Fair use policy can sort out the issue. Still, many times, it has been seen that copyright rules are violated. Review of copyright policies is necessary from time to time and intellectual property laws must be followed while selecting the contents.
5. **Content Assessment and Quality Enhancement:** Due to rapid growth of these resources, the issue of finding out the best relevant resources of best quality is not an easy task on the part of users. While developing these learning resources, it becomes significant to assess educational needs, and accordingly manage the curriculum development processes. To get relevant learning outcomes, relevant content areas for programmes, courses and modules should be prepared. Quality of the contents is although a difficult task but by selecting appropriate quality contents, it can be overcome.
6. **Infrastructure:** For collaboration and sharing of information, high-bandwidth connections with advanced networking capabilities are required. Now institutions are incorporating information and communication technologies (ICT) into their educational programmes in order to serve their students more cost-effectively with high quality learning material. In many developing countries, however, access to hardware, software and connectivity remain challenges.
7. **Lack of Awareness to Use:** Digital illiteracy and lack of OER consultation results into lack of awareness. Faculty involvement, library use and good reading habits can overcome the problem of awareness among students,

There may be many other challenges towards the open educational resources in any higher education structure like the lack of creation of an OER culture at all levels of education, a lack of capacity, language barrier, etc.

Conclusion

Open Educational Resources are good enough to promote the target of free and compulsory education for all and are also helpful in higher education. But awareness towards the OERs is first and foremost requirement. Educators and information professionals can play a vital role in this area. Digital technology has made the scene very comfortable. OERs can be accessed by a large area of population due to its importance in various fields of education.

References

Agropedia 2017. Retrieved at https://agropedia.iitk.ac.in on dated 2 Feb 2017.

Aview 2017. Retrieved at http://aview.in/ on dated 10 June 2017.

Cape Town Declaration 2007. Cape Town Open Education Declaration: Unlocking the Promise of Open Educational Resources. Retrieved from: www.capetowndeclaration.org/read-the-declaration

eGyankosh 2017. Retrieved at www.eGyankosh.ac.in on 11 June 2017.

ePGPathshala Retrieved at www.ePGPathshala on 11 Feb. 2017.

Flexilearn 2017. Retrieved at http://www.ignouflexilearn.ac.in/

Geogebr 2017. Retrieved at https://www.geogebra.org

Higher Education Academy 2017. Retrieved at https://.heacademy.ac.uk/ on dated 12 July 2017.

Hylen, J. 2007. Giving Knowledge for Free: The Emergence of Open Educational Resources. Retrieved from: www.oecd.org/dataoecd/35/7/38654317.pdf

Karnataka Open Educational Resources 2017. Retrieved at karnatakaeducation.org.in/KOER on dated 12 July 2017.

National Digital Library of India 2017. Retrieved at https://ndl.iitkgp.ac.in on 13 July 2017.

Open Education 2017. https://opensource.com/resources/what-open-education

Open Education Resources 2017. Retrieved at http://oer.nios.ac.in/

Open Educational Resources. Report of the Working Group on Open Access and Open Educational Resources. Retrieved at www.knowledgecommission.gov.in on 15 July 2017.

Open Educational Resources: Innovation, Research and Practice Retrieved at https://oerknowledgecloud.org/sites/oerknowledgecloud.org/files/pub_PS_OER-IRP_web.pdf

Singh and Misra 2016. *Higher Education in India at a Glance.* University News, 54(26).

SWAYAM 2017. Retrieved at https://swayam.gov.in/

TESS-India 2017. Retrieved at http://www.tess-india.edu.in/

UNESCO 2002. "Forum on the Impact of Open CourseWare for Higher Education in Developing Countries." Final report. Retrieved 16 July 2017 from: http://unesdoc.unesco.org

Vigyan Prasar DigitalLibrary 2017. Retrieved at http://www.vigyanprasar.gov.in/digilib/)

William and Flora Hewlett Foundation 2010. Education Program: Strategic Plan. Retrieved from: www.hewlett.org/uploads/documents/Education_Strategic_Plan_2010.pd\

8

National Digital Library: An Open Access Platform of E-Resources

Vijay Kumar Bharati

ABSTRACT

Today, digital libraries are being created for diverse communities and in different fields e.g. education, science, culture, development, health, governance and so on. With the availability of several free digital library software packages in the recent times, the creation and sharing of information through the digital library collections has become an attractive and feasible proposition for library and information professionals around the world. This chapter discusses the new activities, methods and technology used in digitization and formation of digital libraries of higher Indian institutions and universities prepared by IIT Kharagpur. The chapter provides on the overview of National Digital Library and point out the browsing way to retrieve information from NDL. This chapter also describes the type of knowledge materials available at the NDL platform. It set out some key points involved and the detailed plans required in this process, and offers advice and guidance for the practising Librarians and Information Scientists. The chapter ends with the characteristics and limitations of NDL.

Keywords: *E-Resources; National Digital Library; ICT; Library; National Mission on Education.*

Introduction

Information and Communication Technology has revolutionized the concept of libraries. Each and every library is slowly getting digitized. Digital Libraries are being created today, for diverse communities and in different fields e.g. education, science, culture, development, health, governance, and so on. A digital library is a collection of digital documents or objects. This definition is the dominant perception of many people today. A digital library is a platform, which is based on digital collection, that is capture, store, preserve and distributes all types of content in digital format (as opposed to print, microform, or other media) and accessible by computers. The digital content may be stored locally, or accessed remotely via computer networks. A digital library is a kind of information retrieval system, whose fundamental purpose to provide access to information along with appropriate reference tools for identifying and evaluating the possible sources and types of information. Nevertheless, Smith (2001) defined a "digital library as an organized and focused collection of digital objects, including text, images, video and audio, with the methods of access and retrieval and for the selection, creation, organization, maintenance and sharing of collection." Though the focus of this definition is on the document collection, it stresses the fact that the digital libraries are much more than a random assembly of digital objects. They retain the several qualities of traditional libraries such as a defined community of users, focused collections, long-term availability, and the possibility of selecting, organizing, preserving and sharing resources.

The digital libraries are sometimes perceived as institutions, though this is not as dominant as the previous definition. The following definition given by the Digital Library Federation (DLF) brings out the essence of this perception. "Digital Libraries are organization that provide the resources, including the specialized staff to select, structure, offer intellectual access to interpret, distribute, preserve the integrity of and ensure the persistence over time of collections of digital works so that they are readily and economically available for use by a defined community or set of communities" (DLF 2001). The point in this definition is on the digital library as a dynamic, and a growing organism. As digital libraries evolve and become the predominant mode of access to knowledge and learning, institutionalization of digital libraries appears to be on the increase. The fourth law of library science is Save the Time of Patron. Time is a major factor for each and every user of the library. Digital library does not follow only the fourth law of library science, in fact, it accept all the fundamental laws of library science. Digital libraries can solve issues of time and space limitations. They can satisfy the information needs of many patrons at the same time. They play a vital role and serve the needs of every patron in different ways. Digital libraries offer a wide range of new access opportunities that are absent in the traditional library, including remote access, 24-hour access, and multiple patrons for single sources. The arrival and proliferation of electronic resources and digital libraries have already influenced and changed the way, academics ions and scholars use print resources and traditional libraries. It has also sparked a new wave of literature on the perceptions and preferences of print and electronic resources. These are some issues and factors for creating digital library.

Ministry of Human Resource Development under its National Mission on Education through Information and Communication Technology has initiated the National Digital Library (NDL) pilot project to develop a framework of virtual repository of learning resources with a single-window search facility. Filtered and federated searching is employed to facilitate focused searching so that learners can find out the right resource with least effort and in minimum time. NDL is designed to hold content of any language and provides interface support for leading vernacular languages (currently Hindi and Bengali). It is being arranged to provide support for all academic levels including researchers and lifelong learners, all disciplines, all popular form of access devices and differently abled learners. It is being developed to help students to prepare for entrance and competitive examination to enable people to learn and prepare from best practices from all over the world and to facilitate researchers to perform interlinked exploration from multiple sources. The pilot project is devising a framework suitable for future scale up with respect to content volume and diversity to become a full-blown National Digital Library of India over time. It is being developed at IIT Kharagpur.

National Digital Library

National Mission on Libraries i.e. High Level Committee, has been set up by Ministry of Culture, Government of India, vide notification no. 18-4/2009_lib (Pt) dated May 4, 2012 in pursuance of National Knowledge Commission recommendations for sustained attention for development of Libraries and Information Science Sector. National Mission on Libraries has set up four working groups and after deliberating the recommendations of the working groups, it formulated the scheme "National Mission on Libraries (NML)—up gradation of libraries providing service to the public". The scheme consists of four components:

- Creation of National Virtual Library of India (NVLI)
- Setting up of NML Model Libraries
- Quantitative and Qualitative Survey of Libraries
- Capacity Building.

The purpose of National Virtual Library of India is to facilitate a comprehensive database on digital resources on information about India and on information generated in India, in an open access environment.

The National Digital Library (NDL) is an all-digital library that will integrate all existing digitized and digital contents across institutions of the nation to provide a single-window access with e-learning facility to different groups of users ranging from primary level to higher education level and even lifelong learners of our country. It will provide educational materials in various languages, in all disciplines, in different forms of access devices and will cater to differently abled learners as well. NDL has been designed to benefit all kinds of users like students (of all levels), teachers, researchers, librarians, library users, professionals, differently abled users and all other lifelong learners. NDL will provide a single window search facility to act as a one-stop solution for all digital resources. Information can be personalized based on the education level, choice of language, difficulty level, media of content and such other factors while other digital libraries may not include all these choices. This is thus, like a 'customised service' provided in a 24 × 7 integrated environment where learners can find out the right resource with least effort and in minimum time.

Objectives and Scope

- Create a 24 × 7-enabled Infrastructure for NDL with single window search facility and to include h/w systems, networks, s/w tools, applications and interoperability standards.
- Harvest IDRs (Institutional Digital Repository) across institutions of the nation to provide integrated access.
- Facilitate selected institutes to disseminate existing content and create new digital content.
- Provide support for immersive E-learning environments at multiple levels spanning across all academic levels—school to college to university to lifelong learning. All disciplines—Science, Arts, Humanities, Engineering, Medical, Law, and all languages used as medium of instruction.
- Support interfaces in vernacular and for differently abled users.

Access to NDL System

The NDL system is accessible to all users for general browsing. However, one needs to register with a user id and password and login using those for accessing some classified materials. You can access the NDL system using any of the browsers mentioned below:

- Google Chrome version 38 or above
- Mozilla Firefox version 40 or above
- Internet Explorer version 10 or above
- Opera version 29 or above
- Safari version 8 or above

An individual or institute can simply type in the URL into a common web browser to access the NDL system. Rendering of some contents may require additional software plug-in to be installed at client end. The NDL project is all about knowledge dissemination and there is no fee attached for accessing the digital library. No special hardware or accessories are required to access NDL. NDL can be accessed from devices like PC, laptop, mobile devices supporting any web browser. However, you will need Internet connectivity to access NDL. NDL is not available through physical media such as CD-ROM. Access to the NDL system is free of charge. However, this will lead the user to the materials which may reside on other institutions' servers. Accessing these will be determined by the policy of those institutions and their access rules. There is no restriction on the accessibility of the NDL system. It can be accessed by an individual or institute member equally well. However, access to full text content in many cases (e.g. Springer publisher content) may require institutional membership. NDL is accessible on mobile devices using a common web browser on any of the operating systems IOS, Android or Windows. We will be continually optimizing the NDL website to provide the best mobile user experience. Access to the NDL system is free of charge. However, this will lead the user to the materials which may reside on other institutions' servers. Accessing these will be determined by the policy of those institutions and their access rules.

Knowledge Material

NDL provides the unique facility of choosing knowledge materials as per the education level of the user. The results retrieved for a query can be filtered based on user's choice of 'educational level'. Upon selecting a specific educational level filter (e.g., UG and PG), the results matching the selection criteria only, will be shown to the user. The ultimate aim is to provide the materials in all vernacular languages. However, this will very much depend on the actual availability of materials in the vernacular. NDL can accommodate materials in any language, though User Interface for Browsing and Searching will initially start with the languages Hindi, English and Bengali and will slowly expand to include other languages. NDL contents will be available in various forms like text, audio, video, etc. The nature of media can be chosen by the user to retrieve the materials in the desired format. NDL harvests data from other sources and guides its users to the respective sources through the creation of metadata to define those items. The responsibility or liability of the contents thus lies with the respective source organizations and NDL is not in a position to authenticate the accuracy of the contents. For any questions regarding the quality of the contents, one is requested to contact the respective content provider. The amount of time it takes to download an article depends on the speed of your Internet connection, the size of the article and the location where it is hosted. Sometimes, it can take few minutes to download a page especially, if the page is rich in graphics. All contents on the web are managed by the site owner. Sometimes, contents are removed or re-organized by the owners. In such situations, we expect the content providers to update the link suitably. Try searching the site that the item was linked to. It could still be available on the website but in a different location.

Metadata is the data that represents contents. Metadata includes information that enables users to identify, discover, interpret, or manage content, such as the name of the author of the work, the date on which it was first created or published, or where the physical object is located. It might also include a description of the content: for example, a brief background on the historical and cultural implications of a work. Metadata may also include hyperlinks that direct users to the actual content on a content partner's website. When you filter down to the actual contents of any item on the NDL system, you can access metadata of the item by clicking on the 'Metadata' tab on the top.

The NDL Metadata envelop has been developed using the commonly used metadata standards like Dublin Core (generic), Learning Resource Metadata Initiative (LRMI) (educational) and Shodhganga (thesis). In this approach, the origin of each element of the metadata is identified by retaining the domain name of the adopted standard (such as "dc" for Dublin Core in case of generic metadata elements, "lrmi" for Learning Resource Metadata Initiative in case of educational metadata elements). The standard is flexible thus ensuring that metadata elements can be appended in future to address nature of contents or learners' requirement that has not been envisaged at this stage. Access to the NDL system is free of charge. However, this will lead the user to the materials which may reside on other institutions' servers. Access to others materials will be determined by the policy of those institutions and their access rules. Use of articles retrieved from NDL will be determined by the rights policy of the content provider and any special rights status of the article, as well as the nature of your use. For example, freedom may be given for the use of an article for academic purpose but the same will necessitate permission if used for commercial purpose. Each metadata record will contain a link to the actual item on the content provider's website. Please access the website to assess the rights status of an individual item.

NDL aims to make its educational materials available to all through metadata. Metadata provides textual information of a content which may be actually hosted on the data provider's server. The actual contents are subject to the copyright laws of the respective data providers as the authors or publishers retain copyright to these works which are used by NDL with permission. Anybody reproducing, redistributing, or making commercial use of these materials is responsible for compliance with the terms and conditions asserted by the copyright holder. Transmission or reproduction of protected items beyond that allowed by fair use as defined in the copyright laws requires the written permission of the copyright owners. The option to save or download an article will depend on the access rights provided by the content provider. Once saved, printing can be done. Sometimes, there could be a limit on the number of pages that can be printed (e.g. upto 100 pages). Once again, this will vary from document for document based on the access rights set by the content owner.

Services

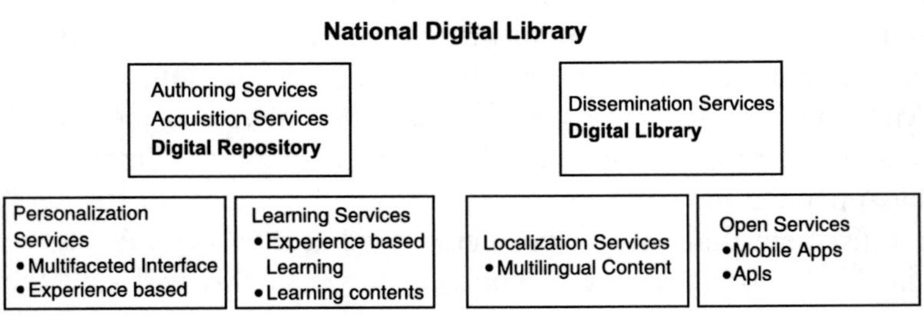

Types of Learning Resources

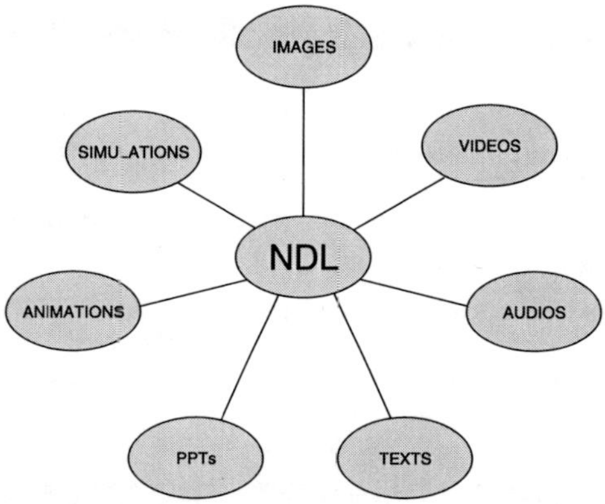

Browsing Data

You can refine your search criteria from the 'Refine search results' facet by choosing different options like author, subject, learning resource type etc. This will help you retrieve an item meeting multiple selection criteria. You can use the 'Advanced Search' option placed on the top right side of the screen to apply multiple selection criteria (*Source*, Educational level, Language, Learning Resource Type) for a more focused and faster search. You can get materials in various forms like video, image, animation, simulation and presentation besides textual materials. Select the 'By Type' option on 'Browse' or the material type from the right hand bar on 'Search' to get materials in your desired form. You can select 'By Subject' from the 'Browse' option and select your subject of interest from the drop down menu. The system will provide you three levels of filtering to refine the subject selection further.

1. **Browsing 'By Type':** Browsing 'By Type' will return items in the form of 'Text', 'Video', 'Image', 'Animation', 'Simulation', 'Audio' or 'Presentation'. You can choose the type of media so that all items of that media type are displayed. The screen has an in-built explanation of the steps to follow.

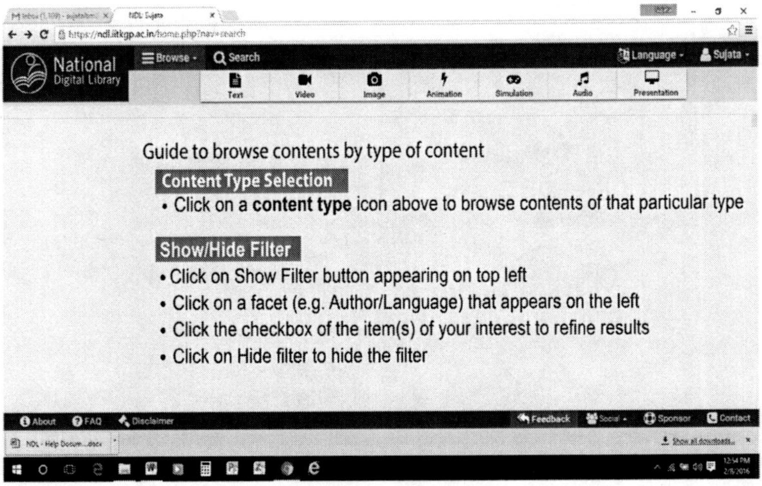

2. **Browsing 'By Subject':** Browsing 'By Subject' will provide three levels of choices that you can make to arrive at your chosen subject. The screen has an in-built explanation of the steps to follow.

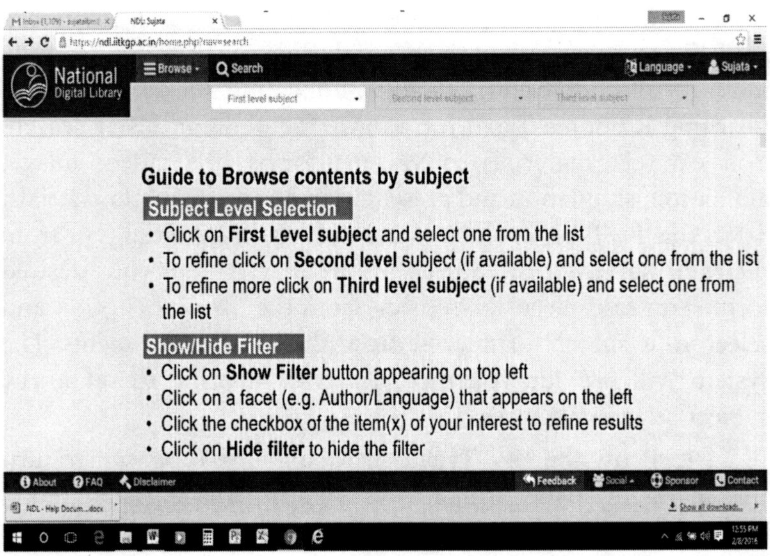

3. **Browsing 'By Source':** Browsing 'By Source' will show a list of institute names, with some important institutes featured on top, so that you can choose your preferred

organization name and browse through all the items from that organization. The screen has an in-built explanation of the steps to follow.

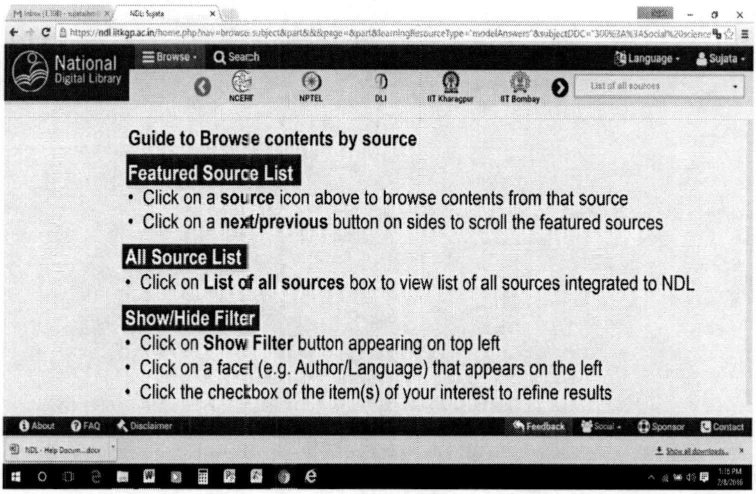

NDL Mobile App

App is an abbreviated form of the word "application." An application is a software program that is designed to perform a specific function directly for the user or, in some cases, for another application program. Recently, NDL has launched an NDL App to access e-resources on your mobile. With the help of installing NDL App, you can access all the resources of NDL on your mobile.

Characteristics, Benefits and Features of Digital Libraries

There are many potential characteristics and benefits of a digital library such as:

- A single window search facility to ever-growing digital content repository.
- Different ways to browse content repository: Browse by content type, Browse by source, Browse by subject and Browse by learning resource type.
- Filtering result of search and browse with facet-based refinement options.

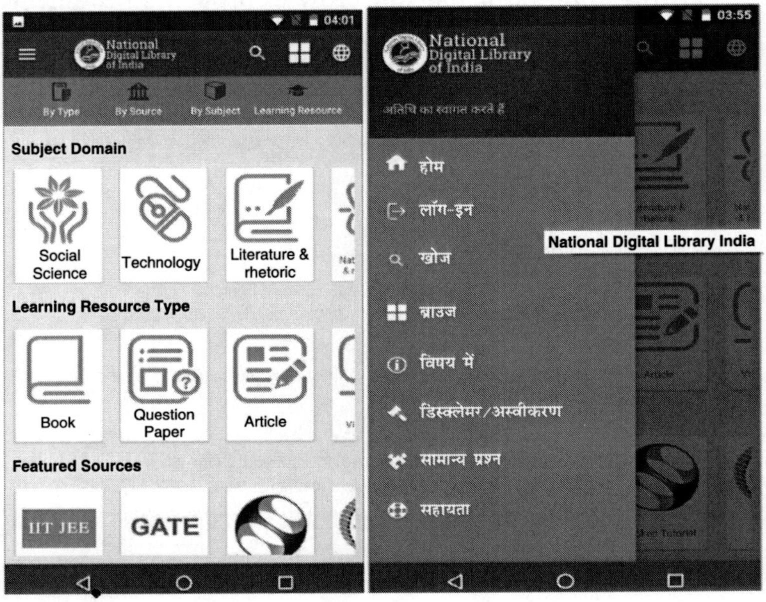

- Contents relevant for different levels of users.
- Contents available for different subject domains: Technology, Arts and Humanities, Social Sciences, Natural Science etc.
- App and content may be accessed in three different languages: English, Hindi and Bengali.
- Ability to access via mobile apps.
- Universal accessibilities.
- Everything can be store.
- Variety of digital information sources.
- Ability to handle multilingual content.
- Digital library reduce the need for physical space.
- Provide new opportunities for the archiving and preservation of all types of content.
- Many patrons can access a particular document at the same time.
- A patron friendly Information Retrieval System.

- Reducing patron dependence on library's print collection.
- Information is always available (24 × 7 hour).
- Free of cost.
- Reliability.
- Easy handling.
- Single windows.
- No need for additional hardware/software.
- No need for trained/technical hand.
- Fit to e-Learning system.

Limitations

- Users have to visit individual websites to access e-resources. No single window search facility for accessing all available digital resources.
- Users need to learn retrieval techniques/search techniques separately as different Digital Library (DL) follows different DL software.
- User interfaces, often, are not interactive, collaborative and participative.
- Few mechanisms are available for differently abled learners.
- Absence of vernacular access and limited contents.
- Knowledge Repository on most subjects are not yet available for scholars.
- Few e-Learning environments for the students and teachers that access information from all available sources.
- Distance mode of learning in India is helping mainly to increase learner-base not the knowledge-base as effectively as needed.
- Non-integration of learner-learner, teacher-teacher and teacher-learner communication tools within learning environment.
- Learning resources are generally outside the integrated learning environment.

References

Borgman, C.L. 1999. What are digital libraries? Competing Visions. Information Processing & Management 35, 227-43.

Croneis, K.S. and Henderson, P. 2002. Electronic and digital librarian positions: A content analysis of announcements from 1990 through 2000. *Journal of Academic Librarianship* 28(4), 232-37.

Digital Library Federation. 1998. A working definition of digital library, retrieved January 16, 2006, websitehttp://www.diglib.org/about/dldefinition.htm

Digital Library Federation. 2001. Registry of Digitized Books and Serial Publication, Available at http://www.digilib.org/collections

http://cairiebird.wordpress.com/

http://dcmsme.gov.in

http://ndl.iitkgp.ac.in/

http://whatis.techtarget.com

Krishna, K.M. and Adwani, N. 2010. Digital information access and its impact on reading habit of users. *SRELS Journal of Information Management*, 47(3), 289-95.

Matson, L.D. and Bonski, D.J. 1997. 'Do digital libraries need librarians? An experimental dialog'. Online 21(6), 87-92.

Smith, Abbey 2001. Strategies for Building Digitized Collection. Washington, D.C. Digital Library Federation, Council on Library and Information Resources. Available at http://www.clir.org

Part III
ICT

9

Open Access Scholarly Communication: Challenges and Opportunities to New ICT Era

Abdul Jalil

ABSTRACT

Scholars always require, access or browse to relevant scholarly literature of their particular field to develop the knowledge further. Increasingly, that literature may be interdisciplinary, expensive, e-resources and worldwide, and hidden behind technical barriers to comply with license or proprietary restrictions. That is also burgeoning; it is little wonder that even in the richest universities a cross the globe, scholars face difficulty in accessing the specialized literature that they need, while those at the poorest barely have any access at all. The open access movement has made it easier to answer all these critical questions. Some of the prominent personalities have shown interest in transforming it, rather, reforming the existing scholarly communication system, and so that, open access can function effectively in the rapidly changing ICT environment.

The chapter discusses the researcher's extent to appreciation of open access scholarly communication. It includes benefits of open access journal as well as the opportunities of open access journal. It has been discussed and suggested that there are so many challenges regarding publishing and accessing of open access scholarly communication. It reveals the open access scholarly communication and the major benefit derived from using it is its free access (no cost) through online medium, which is necessary for research.

Keywords: *Open Access; Scholarly Communication. Scholarly Literature, e-resources, ICT environment.*

Introduction

The information communication technology has perform vital role in this age of information and communication technology. Free flow of information is a basic principle for bridging the knowledge gaps between information rich and information poor community. Social inclusion and economic empowerment are also achieved in a society where citizens have universal access to a information and knowledge, ranging from public information to specialized or customized information related to one's profession, vocation or culture. Open access to information and knowledge is a key contribution in provisioning universal access to information and knowledge. With the availability of ICTs, it continues to make changes in every aspect of our society and reshapes scholarly communication in many ways. The exponential growth of scholarly literature has put a severe hindrance on their accessibility, and the libraries, particularly in the developing countries is vexed with the problem of providing access to vast amount of literature. Moreover, the increase in the prices of academic journals by the publishers has posed a major threat to libraries, which support academic researcher's research activities. To communicate the fruits of scholarly literature to a worldwide community of researchers and scientists, the open access initiative emerged as a revolutionary movement that promotes free access to scholarly journals over the Internet, removes the price and permission barriers and ensures the widest possible dissemination of research. Open access journals and literature are now expected to be read more often than those with subscriptions thereby having a higher impact rates.

Open Access

There are so many definitions of open access given by different information scientist. According to Giarlo, open access as a model of scholarly communication through which users can view, download, open, access, copy and print freely. That includes journal articles, books, conference proceedings etc. that means users are able to access free scholarly materials without any cost, without any barrier, the price of the academician has been born by some funding agencies, government, the author, the authors' research institution.

"Open access" is the term used to describe literature that is available to any reader at no cost on the Internet. The copyright owner—usually the author—allows the user to freely read, download, open, access, copy, print, distribute, search, link to the full text of the article, crawl it for indexing, and use the article for lawful purposes (Kwan, 2003). In open-access journals, authors either retain copyright or are asked to transfer the copyright to the publisher. The only role of copyright in open-access literature is to give authors control of the integrity of their work and the right to be properly acknowledged and cited (Kwan, 2003). Although open access is a concept that is most often applied to online academics, it is nonetheless compatible with print for those journals that also have a printed version. Open access is free of charge for readers of the online version, but does not exclude priced access to print versions of the same work (Ricardo and Mercè, 2004).

The revolution of open access, since early 1990s, has liberated libraries and information centers all over the world. More than ever, librarians are experiencing a rise in prestige because of their ability to contribute to the digital management of information, which somewhat, was being threatened by commercial information providers of the Internet era (Swan, and Chan, 2010).

Examples of open access journals include library philosophy and practices, while Lund University Library has developed a directory of open access journals after the First Nordic Conference on Scholarly Communication in Lund/Copenhagen in 2002.

Open Access Journals

Open access journals are scholarly communications that are available through Internet, without legal, financial, geographical and technical barriers other than that inseparable from gaining access to the Internet itself. Those journals are subsidized but some require amount on behalf of the writer. Subscribed journals are financed by the government research institute or academic research institute, those requiring amount are typically financed, made available to research scholars may also from any funding agencies, that may be government or private funding agency as part of research grant. Those open access journals are have several modifications that they difficult in nature. Considerably, these type of journals are hybrid open access journals and delayed open access journals (Suber, 2009).

Some of the open access journals avenue for direct access include: the Directory of Open Access Journals, the directory of Free Full Text; Free Medical Journals Directory; the High Wire Press; and the Open J-Gate. It is also possible to access open access journal's articles indirectly by using search engines such as Google or Google scholar.

Opportunities with Open Access

Peter Suber (2004) eloquently explains the opportunities of open access that it has many opportunities for all stakeholders, including:

Authors: Open access gives the author a global audience, larger than proprietary-based journals or e-materials.

Publisher: Open access helps the publisher in worldwide, visible, discoverable, retrievable and accessible. In open access, journal articles get more publicity than that of proprietary publisher.

Readers: Open access provide them barrier-free information to the literature they need for their research, not constrained by the budgets of the libraries where they may have access privileges. It increases their convenience, reach, and retrieval power.

Libraries: Open access solves the pricing crisis for scholarly journals. It also solves the permission crisis. Open access serves library's interests in other indirect ways, too. Librarians want to help users, find the information they need, regardless of the budget-enforced limits on the library's own collection. Librarians want to help faculty, increase their audience and impact and thereby, help the university raise its research profile.

Universities: Open access increases the visibility of their faculty and institution, reduces their expenses for journals, and advances their mission to share knowledge.

Funding agencies: Open access increases the return on their investment in research, making the results of the funded research more widely available, more discoverable, more retrievable, and more useful. Open access serves public funding agencies by providing public access to the results of publicly funded research.

Governments: As funders of research, governments benefit from open access in all the ways that funding agencies do. Open access also promotes democracy by sharing government information as rapidly and widely as possible.

Citizens: Open access gives them access to peer-reviewed research (most of which is unavailable in public libraries) and gives them access to the research, for which they have already paid through their taxes. It also helps them indirectly by helping the researchers, physicians, manufacturers, technologists, and others who make use of cutting-edge research for their benefit.

There are various studies which confirmed that an open access article is more likely to be used and cited than one behind subscription barriers. There is enough evidence that open access documents are most likely to be cited than non-open access documents. This gives open access authors an advantage over other authors, who are skeptical about open access. Scholars are paid by research funders and/or their universities to do research; the published article is the report of the work they have done, rather than an item for commercial gain. The more the article is used, cited, applied and built upon, the better for research as well as for the researcher's career (Suber, 2004).

According to Cetto (2001), open access goes beyond the academic circle and spreads its wings to other areas. An open access article can be read by anyone, including professionals, researchers in different fields, media practitioners, politicians, civil servants, etc. Open access articles can often be found with a web search, using any general search engine or those specialized for the scholarly/scientific literature. He stated that librarians believe that open access promises to remove both the price barriers and the permission barriers that undermine library efforts to provide access to journal articles. Most library associations have either signed major open access declarations or created their own. In most universities, the library houses the institutional repository, which provides free access to scholarly work of the university's faculty. Some open access advocates believe that institutional repositories will play a very important role in responding to open access mandates from funders (Cetto, 2001).

Most developing countries cannot afford subscribed journals and books. Most of these journals and books are available internationally, but quite expensive for developing countries standards. This is where open access comes in. In developing countries, researchers, students, and scholars, in general get materials via open access. In this way, they are able to obtain the latest updated materials which were beyond their reach (Hamel, 2005).

Challenges to Open Access

The major problem of publishing and accessing open access journals in developing countries are ICT infrastructure. It is impossible to get benefit from open access journal without proper ICT infrastructure. The developing countries hardly 10% of the population uses Internet, where speed of the Internet or non-connectivity is one of the major constraint. Another challenge is copyright issue. Many research institutes of developing countries have not encouraged the faculty members and research scholars to contribute to open access or access open access materials. On a positive note, some universities like the University of Western Cape have launched an Open Content project in which students and staff participate. Developing countries scholars have continually relied on e-papers from developed countries.

Language is a major barrier in developing countries; each developing country has different official languages. Most of the online literature and open access materials are in English language. Resistance to change has been seen as another challenge. Many librarians, researchers, readers and authors have resisted the change to the e-world. Some of them believe that if they embrace the electronic publications completely, their jobs will be at risk. There are researchers and authors in developing countries who have kept their research findings unpublished due to the fear that others will copy their findings. No wonder an old saying agrees with this, that the richest place on earth is the graveyard, where many unexploited ideas are buried with their owners (Antelman, 2004). Many developing countries, especially some Asian and African countries, lack the infrastructure to handle open access materials. Telecommunication challenges like bandwidth allocation, and weak communication and social infrastructure have not only blocked information flows but ultimately stifled social and economic development. Internet connection is a key to open access. Despite a very rapid rate of the Internet growth, developing countries still lags behind in Internet connectivity with barely 10% of Internets in developing countries and the Middle East. Scientists who are not connected to the Internet are excluded automatically from publishing in, and benefiting from, a growing number of journals, because many new journals are created online while many old ones now, often have online counterparts.

Moreover, it has been said about the information rich and information poor. In other words, there exists a digital divide in the above two distinct worlds. According to DiMaggio et al. (2001), digital divide refers to inequalities in access to the Internet, extent of use, knowledge of search strategies, quality of technical connections and social support, ability to evaluate the quality of information, and diversity of uses. The digital-divide underpins much of the ongoing discourse on whether ICT can be harnessed for mitigating poverty in developing countries with several voices arguing that those who live below poverty line have no need for ICTs. The proponents of ICTs, on the other hand, consider ICTs as tools that can be used to provide the poor with economic opportunities and improvements in human well-being (UNCTAD, 2003).

Although open access offers free access to information, there is a need for some funding to take care of Internet subscriptions, designing of tools, management, and availing technology. Most developing countries' economies are constrained or have other priorities and would invest in open access only, if their budgets have surplus (Raney, 1998).

Suber (2004) listed four major challenges to the success of open access:

- **Filtering and censorship barriers:** Many educational institution, employers, and governments want to limit what users can see.
- **Language barriers:** English is the prime language for most online literature, or just one language, and machine translation is very weak.
- **Handicap access barriers:** Most websites are not yet as accessible to handicapped users as they should be.
- **Connectivity barriers:** Billions of people uses digital divide, including millions of serious scholars, offline.

Conclusion

It is highly recommended that scholars indicated overwhelmingly that they cite open access journals in this new ICT era. This finding is in conformity with what Suber (2004) indicated that researchers cite more open access journal articles than those behind subscription barriers and that the more an article is used, cited, applied, and built upon, the better for research as well as for the researcher's career. It was found that the major benefit derived from using open access journals is that it provides free online access to the literature necessary for research. This indicated that open access journals provide free online access to the literature necessary for one's research. It was also found that unavailability of Internet facilities is a major constraint to the use of open access scholarly publications. This is in conformity with what Suber (2004) stated that connectivity barriers keep billions of people, including millions of serious scholars, offline. Arunachallam (2002) pointed out that the digital divide between the developed and the developing countries need to be closed in order to enhance electronic publishing.

References

Antelman, K. 2004. Do open access articles have a greater research impact? Retrieved 12 May 2012 from: http://eprints.rclis.org/bitstream/10760/5463/1/do_open_access_CRL.pdf

Arunachallam, S. 2002. Reaching the unreached: What role can ICTs play in rural development? Paper presented at the Asian Regional Conference of UNICT Task Force Media Lab Asia (New Delhi, 25 April 2002).

Berlin declaration on open access to knowledge in the science and humanities, 2003. Retrieved 1 May 2012 from: http://www.zim.mpg.de/openaccess-berlin/berlin_declaration.pdf

Bethesda statement on open access publishing 2003. Retrieved 1, May 2012 from: http://www.earlham.edu/~peters/fos/bethesda.htm

I. Oghenetega and Onoriode, Oghenovo Kelvin. Open Access and Scholarly Publishing: Opportunities and Challenges to Nigerian Researchers: *Chinese Librarianship: An International Electronic Journal*, 33. Retrieved May 12, 2015 from URL: www.iclc.us/cliej/cl33IO.pdf

Moller, A. 2004. The rise of open access journals: Their viability and their prospects for the African scholarly community. Paper presented during the International Conference on Electronic Publishing and Dissemination Organized by Council for Development of Social Science Research in Africa (CODESRIA) held from 1-2 September 2003. Retrieved May 9, 2012 from: http://ahero.uwc.ac.za/index.php?module=cshe&action=viewtitle&id=cshe1_2

Srinivasan, Ramesh 2006. Where Information Society and Community Voice Intersect. *The Information Society: An International Journal*, 22(5), Indiana: Taylor & Francis Pub.

Suber, P. 2004. A very brief introduction to open access. Retrieved May 7, 2012 from: http://www.earlham.edu/~peters/fos/brief.htms

10

Information and Communication Technological Based Library and Users Services

Ompal Singh

ABSTRACT

Modernization of libraries in the late 1990s and Web 2.0 technologies of 21st century has totally changed the concept of library services. The introduction of Information Technology (IT) is one of the magnificent gifts of modern science and technology which has brought the tremendous changes in library and information science. Information and Communication Technology (ICT) is the part of Information Technology. Information and communication technology has tremendously changed the house keeping operations (e.g. acquisition, cataloguing, circulation management, and serial control) as well as the way services are delivered. The use of information and communication technologies has become the reason, a transformation in the user's perception from what is being hosted in the library to how and when services are rendered to fulfill their request. Information and communication technology has enabled users to avail many services without any human intervention, the role of library and Information science professionals is changing from an intermediary to a facilitator and enabler. Nowadays, libraries and librarians play a significant role in providing access to information, organizing it, and helping users to find the information they need.

Today, library services depend upon the information and communication technology. This chapter highlights the meaning of information and communication technology, information and communication technological based library and user's services and challenges faced by the professionals in this era.

Keywords: *Information & Communication Technology; based Library & User's Services and Challenges Serial Control, Circulation management.*

Introduction

Library catalogue is the most important tool for locating materials in the library. The emergence of computers, with their ability to process large amount of information and output in a variety of formats has finally brought the library to the users, wherever, they may be located, in the form of Online Public Access Catalogue (OPAC). The computer has become an integral part of information society today. Traditional libraries are improving their roles in the society. The advent of information technology is one of the brilliant gifts of modern science and technology. Library is providing information to their users through the computers and Internet. Modern libraries serve as information needs of the users and supply requisite information. Libraries are complete entities, having large collections and serving a huge clientele to carry out various operations in library effectively. Information and communication technology increases the capabilities of libraries and their professionals to support effective education, learning and research. Information and communication technology survives and makes true laws of library science "Every reader his/her books/information." "Save the time of the readers" and "Library is a growing organism".

Meaning of Information and Communication Technology (ICT)

ICT is the set of technological tools and resources used to communicate and to create, disseminate, store and manage information.

According to Carter (1987), "The system and devices used for receiving, storing, analyzing and communicating information in all its forms, and their application to all aspects of our lives, including the office, the faculty, and home."

According to Hamelink, C.J. (1987), "ICTs are those technologies that enable the handling of information and facilitate different forms of communication. It include capturing technologies (e.g. camcorders), storage technologies (e.g. CD-ROM) processing technologies (e.g. application software), communication technologies (e.g. Local Area Network) and display technologies (e.g. computer monitor)."

Need of ICT in Libraries

Due to the information explosion, it is very difficult to handle large information with traditional library tools like manual catalogue, bibliographies, etc. In today's library environment, providing the right information at the right time and to the right users in the right way, is not possible without ICT application. ICT has become necessity and need.

ICT Based Library Services

Generally, ICT is used in various areas of library activities. Some of the areas where new technologies can perfectly be used are as follows:

Acquisition Section:

- Accession list
- Order file/report

Cataloguing/Classification:

- Catalogue Card/label production
- Retrospective conversion
- On-line catalogue

Circulation Section:

- Issuing
- Inter Library Loan (ILL)
- Reservations
- Over dues

Serial Management:

- Serial check-in/out and cleaning
- Union/holding list

Management Section:

- Accounting/budgeting
- Word processing/mailing
- Scheduling/planning
- Statistics Report

Information Storage/Retrieval:

- Database construction
- Online database searching
- Downloading/uploading
- Indexing and abstracting

Reference/Information services:

- Bibliographic listings
- Library instructions
- Public access/computer literacy.

ICT Based Users Services in the Library

Due to information explosion, information are coming out in electronic format. Some library users are adopting electronic habits, making large use of the new ICT based computers, the Internet, intranet, extranet and other technologies. As a result, library users are placing daily, new demands on their libraries. They require access to the latest information, updated information resources, and access to ICT facilities that they could use in their work.

Nowadays, the use of ICT in libraries enhances user's satisfaction. The use of ICT provides various benefits to library users.

- ICT provides unlimited information from different sources.
- ICT provides the information easily and speedily.
- ICT facilitated the reforming and combining of data from different sources.
- ICT provides remote access to users.
- ICT provides round the clock access to users.

With the help of ICT, libraries are also providing various ICT based services to the users which are as under:

Web 2.0

Web 2.0 is the term, given to describe a second generation of the World Wide Web (WWW) that focuses on the ability of people to collaborate and share information online. Web 2.0 basically refers to the transition from static HTML web pages to a more dynamic web that is more organized and is based on serving web applications to users. Other improved functionality of web 2.0 includes open communication with an emphasis on web-based communities of users and more open sharing of information. Over time, web 2.0 has been used more as a marketing term than a computer science-based term. Blogs, Wikis & web services are all seen as components of web 2.0.

Web Access to OPACs

With the help of web-based Online Public Access Catalogue (OPAC) users can learn how to use one universal access client, the web browser.

Online Instructions

The web browsers are helping librarians implementing online-based bibliographic or library use programs. It provides various online materials on searching online resources and virtual tours of library collections.

Electronics Document Delivery

ICT-based services has become helpful to the libraries to deliver the copies of journals and other documents in digital format mainly in portable document format (PDF) to the library users.

Web 2.0 Tools and Applications:

Web tools are:

Wikis

It is powerful content management system. It allows any one to add a new article or revise an existing article through a web browser. It is an ideal for students, researchers, and support staff for collaborative work allowing focus and content. Wikis are as knowledge management tools. They works as public knowledge repositories.

Flickr

It is a social network for showing photos. With the help of Flickr, users can work together to photo projects and use each other's tags to find new photos. Flickr enables users to contribute organize, share and discuss photos.

Podcast

The podcast like broadcast, is a series of digital media files which are distributed over the Internet using syndication feeds for playback on portable media players and computers.

Challenges of Using ICT in Libraries

- Lack of fund for ICT infrastructures.
- Power interruption.
- Insufficient bandwidth.
- Even change of hardware and software.
- Lack of IT expert staff.
- Copyright and Intellectual Property Rights Management.

Conclusion

Information and Communication Technology has changed the entire environment of libraries. The provision and the use of information and communication technology is a part and parcel of the entire system, to the students, information and science professionals and the institution. With the aid of the information and communication technology, libraries are actually marching towards achieving the goal of providing pinpointed, exhaustive, and expeditious information services which are more convenient, better accessible and cost effective. Information science professionals have modern digital technologies and their applicability to knowledge handling activities that have helped in distributing qualitative services to the end users. Information and communication technology has reduced the library from its stature as custodian of our library heritage to bring competitors among many others in the information society. The technological tools of information age such as computer networks, library networks (DELNET, INFLIBNET), digital information resources, and databases, available in the libraries have put an unprecedented volume of information at finger tips.

References

Arora, Jagdish 2001. "Web-based digital resources and services: Trends and innovation. In creation and management of digital resources." Paper presented at the Eighth National Convention for Automation of Libraries in Education and Research Institute (CALIBER-2001) Pune, March 15-16, 2001. Edited by MKR Naidu and others, Ahmedabad: INFLIBNET Centre.

Chauhan, Buddhi Prakash 2004. ICT enabled library information services: Winter School on ICT enabled library and information services. TIET Patiala, pp. 28-35.

Chisenga, J. 2004. ICT in Libraries: An overview and general introduction to ICT in libraries in Africa." Paper presented at INASP ICT workshop, held at Johanesberg, South Africa on July 21-23, 2004. Available: http://www.inasp.info/lsp/ict-workshop-2004/seassional-chisenga

Devarajan, G. 2005. *Applied Research in Library and Information Science*. New Delhi, Ess Ess Publications, 2005.

Hamelink, C.J. 1997. New Information and Communication Technology: Social Development and Cultural Changes. Discussion paper, UNRISD, Geneva.

Islam, Md. Shariful and Islam Md. Nazmul 2006. Information and Communication Technology in Libraries: A New Dimension in Librarianship." *Asian Journal of Information Technology* 5(8): pp. 809-17, 2006. Medwell Online, 2006.

Kumar, P.S.G. 2003. *Information Technology: Basics Concepts*. New Delhi, B.R. Publishing Corporations.

Mayega, Stephen, "Library Information Services in the Digital Age." Eprint.reclis.org/12567/2/paper.pdf

Tariq, Asraf 2004. *Library Services in Electronic Environment: Changes, Challenges, Issues and Strategies*. New Delhi, Kaveri Books.

Vinitha, K. Kanthimathi 2006. Impact of Information and Communication Technology on Library and Its Services. ICT Conference on Digital Learning Environment. 11-13 January. Bengaluru.

11

Emerging Trends in Library and Information Science: Challenges and Opportunities in the ICT Era

Sandhya Aggarwal

ABSTRACT

The user wants to locate information with one click. Students today use iphone, ipad and so on, and wants to access all information anywhere and anytime. It has become a challenge for librarians that how can they satisfy the changed needs of the users in less time. Librarians have to take initiative and become self-dependent, as per the need of the hour. Managing e-resources are critical, whether you are new or have been engaged in it for years? They should take these new trends and challenges as new opportunities, as how can they make use of this technology better access of information. Social media, e-books, e-journals etc. can be very useful, if librarians use them effectively.

Keywords: *ICT; E-Resources, Structuration Social Media, Knowledge Creator.*

Introduction

With the advent of Information and Communication Technology (ICT), there has been a significant impact on Library and Information Centres (LICs) that has further paved way in modernizing them in different ways. The management of obsolete knowledge and technology in the current knowledge and technology for the future is the great challenge as shown in the example of Floppy Disk.

Floppy > CD-ROM > Pendrive > Mobile > Palm Digital Assistants

Review of Literature

1. Blackburn, Heidi (2011) observed in his study that libraries have increasingly seen technology become a quick candidate as a solution to nearly every problem existing in the field. Though rapidly suggested as an alternative, the new technology is not adopted as quickly as in other sectors. However, Millennials act as change agents and bring technology-driven attitudes to work, using specific communication channels to change employee attitudes towards adoption of the new tools.
2. Siddike, AbulKalam (et al.) (2011) explores the extent of adoption of information and communication technology (ICT) in the university libraries of Bangladesh. The chapter discusses the present conditions of using ICT by the public and private university libraries in Bangladesh and finds the problems faced by the professionals and made some specific recommendations for the solutions.
3. Weiner, Sharon Gray (2003) studied that libraries are affected by discontinuous change caused by the type and rapidity of technological innovations. By examining the theories of structuration, diffusion of innovation, and contingency, change in libraries can be better understood, thus easing its adoption and assimilation. There is a need to reconceptualise libraries.

Objectives

1. To highlight the new technology and tools for libraries.
2. To show the problem faced by the library staff in adopting new technology.
3. To highlight the necessity for organising various training programme, workshop etc. for librarians.

New Trends of Technology

1. E-books
2. E-Readers
3. Mobile Computing

4. Cloud Computing
5. Web 2.0
6. E-Learning
7. Library 2.0
   - 7.1 Wikis
   - 7.2 Instant Messaging
   - 7.3 Blog
   - 7.4 RSS
   - 7.5 Streaming Media
   - 7.6 HTML Feeds
   - 7.7 Podcasting
   - 7.8 Vodcasting
   - 7.9 SMS Enquiry Service
   - 7.10 Collaborative Service Platforms
     - 7.10.1 Social Networks
     - 7.10.2 Tagging
     - 7.10.3 Social Bookmarking Services
   - 7.11 Mashup
   - 7.12 Ajax (Asynchronous JavaScript and XML)
   - 7.13 API

What are the Changes from Traditional Library to Digital Library

- Print to digital information: E-Books, E-Journals, etc.
- Catalogues: Card Catalogue to Online/web OPAC
- Security of Library books: Cameras, Barcodes > Magnetic wire > RFID Tags
- Print journals to online/electronic journals
- Library Access in real time
- Post to E-Mail
- Websites
- Spines to Barcodes
- E-Stockverification: Manual to E-Stockverification
- Circulation: Issue and return of books from manual to computerized.

Challenges and Opportunities

1. **Inadequate funds:** If we want any technical support in open source software, then the charges for this are very high which any library cannot afford.
2. **Lack of computer knowledge:** Computer is necessary in every field like business, administration, banking etc. But many professionals like seniors don't know how to use the computer. They prefer manual working for their convenience.
3. **Internet connectivity:** There is need of full speed Internet service, but this broadband connectivity is frequently interrupted. It affects the work in a harmful manner.
4. **Cost of infrastructural development:** Various tools and infrastructure are required for any new technique i.e. computer, furniture, manpower, etc for which the budget became high.
5. **Lack of skilled manpower:** Library staff should be trained, if the libraries adopt new technology, users don't know about this and in that, case library staff guides the user.
6. **Lack of ICT-related knowledge:** Every staff in any library don't know about the ICT-related knowledge like today is the trend of open source software, if we adopt a open source software to manage the knowledge, then we should know the downloading and installation of operating system, Linux, commands of Linux, Various computer languages: HTML, SQL, C etc.
7. **Lack of ICT training program:** Training program for professional improvement should be organized.
8. Lack of awareness of ICT potential by users.
9. Poor attitude of staff towards library automation.
10. Balancing the "old" and the "new".

References

Blackburn, Heidi. 2011 Millennials and the Adoption of New Technologies in Libraries through the Diffusion of Innovations Process" Criss Library Faculty Publications. Paper 8. http://digitalcommons.unomaha.edu/crisslibfacpub/8

Lalitha, P. 2008. Impact of information and communication technology on changing scenario of library and information centres. Current trends in libraries in the digital era, edited by Rhoda Bharucha, Ahmedabad: Ahmedabad Management Association, pp. 11-21.

Siddike, Abul Kalam and Munshi, M. Nasiruddin and Sayeed, M. Abu 2011. The Adoption of Information and Communication Technology (ICT) in the University Libraries of Bangladesh: An Exploratory Study" Vision 2021: Conference Proceeding. pp. 153-64.

Weiner, Sharon Gray 2003. "Resistance to Change in Libraries: Application of Communication Theories" Libraries and the Academy, 3(1), pp. 69-78.

12

Application of Mobile Technology in Libraries

Vaishali M. Choudhari

ABSTRACT

Today, technologies have become integral part of everyone's life. They are inseparable from each other. The various technology utilized equipments are computer, mobile phones, multimedia, software, games and apps. E-mails, blogs, instant messaging, social networks, twitter and video conference are forms of technology mediated communications. Today, mobile phones are essential part of our life and they are changing the way one connects and interacts with the world. The chapter discusses the application of mobile technology in libraries and its services.

Keywords: *Technology, Mobile, Libraries, Services, etc.*

Introduction

Libraries have always set examples of experimenting with new technology developments whether it is automation or adopting other information and communication technologies to improve the services. Both libraries and technology are growing organisms. Dynamic nature of technology has significant impact on every aspect of modern life. Advent of information and communication technology has provided faster access to information and that's why it is a challenge for libraries to rethink and remodel library services by adopting the technological changes.

Mobile technology is developed for communication purpose. Since last decade, mobile phones have changed the way of life and work. Mobile phones have gained importance throughout the world.

Mobile phones are gaining more popularity among youth. Students are very interested in learning and using these technologies. They access whatever information they required through mobile phones. Most of them are using Internet to stay connected all the time. Social networking apps. like whatsapp, facebook etc. are not only popular among students but also throughout the society.

What is Mobile Technology?

Mobile technology is exactly what the name implies—technology that is portable. Examples of mobile IT devices include:

- laptop, tablets and net book computers
- 'smart phones'
- global positioning system (GPS) devices
- wireless debit/credit card payment terminals.

Mobile devices can be enabled to use a variety of communications technologies, including:

- Wireless fidelity (Wi-Fi)—a type of wireless local area network technology
- Bluetooth—connects mobile devices wirelessly
- 'third generation' (3G), 'fourth generation' (4G), global system for mobile communications (GSM) and general packet radio service (GPRS) data services—data networking services for mobile phones
- dial-up services—data networking services using modems and telephone lines
- virtual private networks—secure access to a private network.

It is, therefore, possible to network the mobile device to home, office, or the Internet while travelling.

Present Scenario of Communication

There is wide range of mobile computing platforms in the market from smart phones to multimedia phones with different types, styles, models and with many inbuilt features and capabilities likes cameras, touch screens, bar code scanning, Wi-Fi, Bluetooth, instant messaging, GIS/GPS, RFID, operating system varying additional storage space, etc. Revolutionary iphone and smart phones (3G and 4G) can be used to run many software applications including Internet access with faster connection speeds. Availability of automatic configuration of GPRS-enabled mobile phones, which help the subscribers to be come online with few clicks.

Emerging technologies like speech technologies in mobile phones have enabled the disabled persons to use mobile effectively.

The M-Learning Development in India

'Libraries in hand' are the latest slogan of the Indians' libraries. People in India have an insatiable thirst for information and knowledge. Moreover, mobile services in India are quite affordable; hence, even an ordinary person can own and use a mobile phone. Added to this fact, India happens to have its large population in the age group of 18 to 20 years.

Technology is vital in today's world and makes everything easier. It has transformed our ways of communicating, socializing, playing, shopping and everything we do. These profound changes are putting increased pressure on the traditional models of teaching and learning. Due to ever increasing and diversified needs of the students, technological advancements are also taking place in the field of education every day. While e-learning is still being used as a supplementary tool to the conventional forms of learning, a new method of knowledge addition called m-learning has emerged in the global scenario.

M-Learning refers to the provision of education and training involving portable or mobile device such as smart phones, personal digital assistant, palmtops, I-pods, digital camera, pocket computers, mobile phones etc. Mobile device provides significant opportunities to help learners become more autonomous and also have the potential to change the delivery of teaching and learning in higher education. Mobile learning process can both complement and conflict with the formal education processes. On the positive side, learners can extend their classroom learning activities to homework, field trips and museum visits by reviewing teaching materials on mobile devices and/or collecting and analyzing information using handled data probes. Liak (2011) believes that mobile learning is about changing the way we teach with the way student's best learn.

In India, total users of telephone (wireless and landline) are 1058.01 million till May 2016. India's telecommunication system is the second largest in the world and in terms of Internet usage, India is third largest in the world next to China and United States. Nowadays 3G mobile users are shifted to 4G device for effective multimedia based m-Learning. Major mobile manufacturers such as Nokia, Sony Ericson and Motorola have linked up with service providers like Airtel, Vodafone and others to provide mobile content, which also include learning content.

Library Services that can be Provided via Mobile Technology

- **SMS notification services:** Libraries may provide the alerts on latest news, events and notices via SMS and MMS to the users wherever they might go. The users can get notified instantly with notice alerts on bringing new books to the notice of users for suggestion, intimation of arrivals of intended documents of users, informing availability of reserved documents for collection, appraising about overdue books, outstanding fines, reminders to return library items, renew books, library circulars, e-journals subscribed, change in timing, information about important events etc.

  Such alert notifications can be generated automatically using integrated library management system software. SMS messages can be sent to group of users simultaneously through many free applications, and intermediary websites/clients.

- **Formal education, distance learning and E-Learning:** Students are very versatile in using their mobile phones and various mobile applications. Academic libraries can harness the advantage of implementing of library services through mobile device to support distance learning, formal education, and research activities in e-learning environment by making the information resources ubiquitous. Library services should also blend with teaching and research practice of colleges/ universities, scientific community or other patrons whom they serve.

- **Database browsing:** Libraries provide access to a variety of its resources and databases. The users can just enter search terms and see results that are designed specifically for mobile viewing. This service includes OPAC (Online Public Access Catalogue), integrated search, and original document search. OCLC's Worldcat mobile application pilot allows users to search for and find books and other materials available in their local libraries through a web application they can access from a PDA or a smart phone.
- **My library:** My library is a personal library space where users can find information and resources of their choice. Users can read alerts, check records, renew resources, request items, track interlibrary loan and document delivery requests, set up email notice of new books and journal's articles, set up reference for catalogue searching, etc.
- **E-Resources with mobile interfaces:** Some publishers are already delivering e-books that are accessible via mobile phones. It offers access to a variety of databases and digital resources. A large collection of audio books, both free and subscription based services are available for download and also transferable to mobile devices. Libraries can make use of multimedia messaging service (MMS) on mobile device to share photos, videos and audio. Most of the e-books publishers provide 24 × 7 accesses to the library subscription from any Internet terminal within the campus, as well as on mobile devices, such as iPads, Android device and Kindle.
- **Library guide:** Libraries can give users the best of library guide information such as library use guide, question answering service and library statistics delivering rich content in a way that works best for users. If users

have questions, and want to contact the librarian for help, they can get a fast response from the library via the mobile device and find the appropriate information needed.

- **Mobile document supply:** The mobile environment and technology presents new opportunities for sending document requests and scanned images, and monitoring the use of collections as well as the automation of administrative operations. It can support electronic fund transfer; supply chain management, e-marketing, online marketing, and online transaction processing, electronic data interchange and automated inventory management systems.
- **Text reference service:** If the library receives high volume of enquires, that slows down the responses, such as dictionary definitions, facts or service information then librarians can provide instant answers, and links to articles/references in real time.
- **Library virtual/audio tours:** Library virtual/audio tours, instruction/induction/orientation programs have been quite significant in bringing the non-users to libraries and also help the remotely located or users located in different geographical locations. Library users, who don't have time to attend on-site workshops, can get access to library tours on their mobile device.
- **QR codes on mobiles:** QR codes stands for 'quick response' and basically two dimensional bar codes that can contain any alphanumeric text and often used to store url's, text, etc., known as mobile tagging.

Skills Required for the Library Staff

Librarians should acquire and apply the following skills, if they wish to provide mobile based services:

Skills relating to training and user orientation to market these services to the users.

Skills for interacting with users via smart phone applications, mobile friendly web pages and third party intermediary clients.

Knowledge of hardware and software of mobile devices.

Develop expertise in protecting privacy and security levels as more personalized information is involved in using for library services.

Familiarity with Internet/intranet services like using emails, SMS and spam preventing etc.

Create mobile optimized content including interactive and participative library homepage, OPAC, virtual tours, and databases.

Conclusion

Mobile Technology has become a very important part of our lives nowdays. Mobile phones were developed primarily for communication purpose. Mobile phones have gained importance in both the developed and the developing countries. The mobile phones are a device that enables users to communicate, connect, transact and innovate. Mobile device and mobile technologies have potential to facilitate teaching and learning process in a great way. Now, students can access a wide range of digital resources and library services and truly engage in learning activities using any mobile device wherever and whenever they choose, not just at their desktops PCs. The impact of mobile technology implementation raised strong awareness amongst library staff for the need to acquire skills to realize the associate benefits.

India may be come one of the leading countries in the adoption of m-learning technology in coming years, owing to the number of young users involved in multimedia mobile usage. The Indian educational industry is evolving. The shift from d-learning to e-learning, and now, from e-learning to m-learning will be the next big wave, which will revolutionize education in India. M-learning will bring about a paradigm shift from the traditional methods of education delivery and integrate ICT as an essential component in everyday learning. Indian libraries are needed to be indispensible their users, and for this, they have to include mobile device as a part of their strategic thinking. Mobile libraries have to grow, and this requires greater collaboration between academic industry, corporations and government. In the current scenario, mobile libraries have the potential to proliferate, and we will witness a situation in which the mobile will definitely be used as a tool to spread learning across the country.

References

Archana, S., and Dr. Yadav, R. 2013. Impact of Mobile Technology on Libraries: A Descriptive Study. *International Journal of Digital Library Services*, 3(4), 1-13.

Boy, I., and Motteram, G. 2013. Does Mobile learning need to move? Global prespective on Computer Assissted Language Learning (pp. 32-35). Glasglow: Glasglow conference proceedings.

Bruce, W. (2011, January 15). USA; Dublin, Ohio. Retrieved December 30, 2016, from https:// www. researchgate.net/publication// library/2011/washburn-io.pdf

Khan, I. 2013. Library, Librarian and Library Services in Web 2.0 Environment. *International Journal of Digital Library Services*, 3(4), 14-18.

Kumbhar, S., and Pawar, R. 2015. Retrieved January 9, 2017, from Researchgate website: https:// www. researchgate.net/publication/

Mill, K. 2009. M-Libraries: Information on the move. England: University of Cambridge.

Mohamed, A., and Gill, N. 2008. M-Libraries: libraries on the move to provide virtual access. Proceeedings of the First International m-libraries Conference (pp. 1-13). London.

Mohan Lal, V., and Shyam, M. 2013. Use of Mobile and Wireless Technology in Indian Libraries. *International Journal of Engineering and Computer Science*, 2(6), 1799-1804.

S.M., and P.K. 2013. Application of Mobile Technologies to Libraries. DESIDOC *Journal of Library and Information Technology*, 33(5), 361-66.

Srinivas, R.N., and Brahmaiah, G. 2016. Mobille Library Services and Technologies: A Study. *International Journal of Research in Library Science*, II (2), 59-66.

Part IV
INSTITUTIONAL REPOSITORY

13

Institutional Repository in the Digital Library

Devendra Kumar Sharma

ABSTRACT

The institutional repositories are themselves repositories, and have always dealt in the management of repositories for their users. With libraries now routinely managing repositories of various types in digital format, it describes mean and qualify 'repository' with 'institutional'? The approach which has now, proved its importance and began to gain ground for research outputs is also now being used for other types of materials which are generated within the institutions. The relation of research generation by academics, with output management by librarians, have created a new form of publication, with open values, which presents a growing challenge to the commercial publishers who have controlled research publication for many decades. Commercial publishers operate on the assumption of a profit motive both for themselves as well as for their authors.

Keywords: *Institutional Repository, Digital Library Output Management, Commercial Publishers.*

Introduction

We begin by looking at the concept of institutional repositories within the broader context of digital libraries. 'Digital libraries' can mean many things, but we consider them to be the libraries first and foremost, and assume that they built upon the enduring principles of information management which have lain at the heart of the practice of librarianship for hundreds of years. We will take at the significance of the qualification which defines the scope of this paper—the institutional repository. With libraries now routinely managing repositories of various types in digital format, what does it mean to qualify 'repository' with 'institutional'?

Keywords: *Institutional, Repository, Digital, Library.*

What is an Institutional Repository?

There are a number of definitions for "institutional repository" (IR). Here are a few key ones:

Clifford Lynch, "Institutional Repositories: Essential Infrastructure for Scholarship in the Digital Age"

A university-based institutional repository is a set of services that a university offers to the members of its community for the management and dissemination of digital materials created by the institution and its community members. It is most essentially, an organizational commitment to the stewardship of these digital materials, including long-term preservation where appropriate, as well as organization and access or distribution.

Mark Ware, Pathfinder Research on Web-based Repositories, "An institutional repository (IR) is defined to be a web-based database (repository) of scholarly material which is institutionally defined (as opposed to a subject-based repository); cumulative and perpetual (a collection of record); open and interoperable (e.g. using OAI-compliant software); and thus collects, stores and disseminates (is part of the process of scholarly communication). In addition, most would include long-term preservation of digital materials as a key function of IRs."

Raym Crow, The Case for Institutional Repositories: A SPARC Position Paper: "Institutional repositories...digital collections capturing and preserving the intellectual output of a single or multi-university community provide a compelling response to two strategic issues facing academic institutions. Such repositories."

> Provide a critical component in reforming the system of scholarly communication, a component that expands access to research, reasserts control over scholarship

by the academy, increases competition and reduces the monopoly power of journals, and brings economic relief and heightened relevance to the institutions and libraries that support them; and have the potential to serve as tangible indicators of a university's quality and to demonstrate the scientific, societal, and economic relevance of its research activities, thus increasing the institution's visibility, status, and public value.

Digital Libraries in a Digital World

In the past decade the concept of the 'digital library' (or the 'electronic library') has been increasingly used, and now crops up relentlessly in the professional literature. This is not surprising, as the combination of low-cost computing and high-speed networking now affects all areas of life in the developed world. 'Digital banking', 'online shopping' and 'digital television' are transforming the ways in which we transact our daily business and consume entertainment. We also book holiday's online, gamble on the Internet and conduct hundreds of other activities online. Increasing numbers of people are working from home, using telecommunications to recreate their office environments in virtual space. As content goes online, and the means of access to it becomes as available and familiar as clicking on the television set, so it is a natural expectation that libraries too will join the interconnected web world.

Institutional Repository in a Disaggregated Publishing Model

Reviewing how this disaggregated publishing model is evolving will helps us to appreciate fully, both the role that institutional repositories that they are playing in such a structure and the impact changes might have on principal stakeholders. This exercise is not futuristic speculation: many of the functional components described below already exists in practice, and as these components proliferate, the model will become richer and more robust. Critical mass in terms of the underlying content repositories that fuel the system represents the single most important element of the new model. Institutional repositories will prove essential in getting the reconstituted scholarly communications structure to a tipping point where the benefits of the new system can be fully realized.

Repository Locus: Institution vs. Discipline

When we talk about 'institutional repository', we use 'institution' to refer the educational or research establishment which is the library's parent body. Institutional repositories have emerged from universities, but are spreading into other types of educational organizations too, such as colleges and research institutes. However, research repositories were until quite recently based only around disciplines. arXiv (www.arxiv.org), was the first and still the best-known disciplinary repository which had emerged as a repository of research papers in particle and high-energy physics, based originally at the Los Alamos National Laboratory. arXiv has been running for some 15 years, and is widely used by physicists across the world. Over time, it has expanded its coverage to embrace associated disciplines such as mathematics and computer science, and it has also changed its physical location, moving to Cornell University Library, a few years ago.

There are significant differences in the ways in which academicians and researchers work in different domains. For the purposes of managers of institutional repositories, the most significant relate to the place of peer review—the process of 'refereeing' by which research is validated by peer experts, or referees, and thereby permitted to enter the discourse and body of knowledge of a particular knowledge domain. What all domains hold in common is their need for peer review, if only to allow the researchers to point to citations in reputable journals in order to prove their credibility in the field, and to enhance their career prospects. Physicists, however, tend to be happy to have their research papers.

The major consequence of the OAI is the appearance of hundreds of institutional archives, alongside the disciplinary archives which continue to exist all over the globe.

IR as a Major Benchmark of Digital Scholarship

IR proponent Lynch (2003) regards institutional repositories as essential infrastructure for modern scholarship. He argues that "the development of institutional repositories emerged as a new strategy that allows universities to apply serious, systematic leverage to accelerate changes taking place in scholarship and scholarly communication". Also, Markey et al. (2007) remarked that, "a considerable portion of the scholarly record is born digital, and some scholarship is produced in digital formats that have no physical, in-the-hand counterparts. The proliferation of digital scholarship raises serious and pressing issues about how to organize, access, and preserve it in perpetuity. The response of academic institutions has been to build and deploy institutional repositories (IRs) to manage the digital scholarship, their learning communities produce."

Repositories and Digital Libraries

Academic libraries, today, are increasingly involved with the digital library agenda represented at conferences such as JCDL because they see that there is a need to develop institutional digital libraries alongside subject-based digital libraries. The institutional library needs a presence on the web—a place to describe its print and web-based services, and to bring together the content, it makes available to its users. It needs to present its catalogue but also its other finding aids—to its collections of e-journals, its collections of digitised materials from its treasures, and other lists which are most usefully presented separately, such as electronic reserve texts or past exam papers. Institutional libraries also are growing the range of services they can offer via their website. Examples of these includes interlibrary loan request—sometimes, by electronic full-text delivery; requests to retrieve store items; book loan renewals and electronic reference support. In addition, library services need to be distributed out to other useful environments, such as student virtual learning environments and university portal sites. They need to be 'skinned' in various ways, and to be capable of being searched in an aggregated and in a user-defined sub-aggregated fashion.

Benefits of an IR

The benefits of repositories to institutions and individuals are numerous and can be grouped into the following categories (Pickton and Barwick (2006)):

Specific to the University, an IR Offers

- Increasing visibility and prestige. A high profile IR may be used to support marketing activities to attract high quality staff, students and funding.
- Centralization and storage of all types of institutional output, including unpublished literature.
- Support for learning and teaching. Links may be made with the virtual teaching environment and library catalogues.
- Standardization of institutional records. The compilation of an 'Institutional CV' and individual online dossiers linked to the full text of articles becomes possible.
- Ability to keep track of and analyse research performance.
- Breaking down of publishers' costs and permissions barriers.
- Alleviation of requirement to trust publishers to maintain information in the long-term, without any commercial benefit for the authors.
- Promotion of a philosophy of wider communication.

Specific to Authors, an IR Enhances

- Dissemination and impact of scholarship. Some studies have estimated that open access articles are cited 50% to 250% more than non-open access articles. In some disciplines, online files receive on average 300% more citations than materials available only in paper format (The Open Citation Project, 2004). Also, Google Scholar gives preferential treatment to materials in IRs; a paper picked up from an IR would appear higher up on the Google results list (Ashworth 2006).
- Storage and access to a wide range of materials. Many authors lack time, resources, or expertise to ensure preservation of their scholarly work. Through an organizationally based IR strategy, long-term accessibility and greater security of work is assured. Research items get a permanent URL compared to a personal or departmental website.

- Feedback and commentary from users. Authors are able to receive and respond to commentary on 'pre-prints'.
- Added value services; such as hit counts on papers, personalised publication lists and citation analyses.
- A central archive of a researchers work.
- A researcher's profile.
- Benefits to researchers and their institutions in terms of prestige, prizes and grant revenue.

Specific to Society/Community

As scholarship is shared, society at large benefits. Maximising public access to research findings online, word in turn, maximises its visibility, usage and impact. It also maximises its benefits to research itself (and hence to the society that funds it) in terms of research dissemination, application and growth, research productivity and progress (ePrints website FAQ, n.d.). Also more sponsors of funded research now have mandates for authors to deposit their articles and other research outputs as a condition for funding. Some policies promote Open Access for funded research. These requirements are intended to increase readership, re-use and dissemination of research outputs. The message to researchers is that the research is incomplete until the output is widely disseminated.

Repositories of Research Papers

Repositories are simply databases, and what distinguishes institutional repositories is the idea that an internal database can serve more than an administrative purpose, and can constitute a building block in a distributed international service which is a virtual database composed of a user-defined set of cooperating databases on the network. This is, therefore, an essentially subversive technology, capable of allowing grassroots publishing by non-publishers, and delivering a service with the same functionality and feel as large as commercially published databases. The idea is not unique. The UK's Joint Information Systems Committee (JISC) funded a number of 'CLUMPS' projects as part of the Electronic Libraries Programme (eLib) in the late 1990s. These created federated databases of academic library catalogues. However, that was a more straightforward undertaking, as the library catalogues involved were already central university services, available to the outside world for searching over the Internet.

Repositories of Other Objects

In its seminal analysis of trends in the library and information world published in 2003, the Online Computer Library Center (OCLC) reported on feedback obtained from surveying librarians and users about the relevance of libraries to digital content. One response highlights the need for librarians to address new custodial challenges:

> Librarians are way too focused on published material: they should leave that to the Amazons and concentrate on the hard stuff. (Online Computer Library Center, 2004)

By 'hard stuff' might be meant, the types of content which are generated in academic institutions but which are not destined for publication. There are three reasonably well-known examples of such types of content, though the potential clearly exists for many further types that may have a more limited appeal as a part of distributed services.

Learning Objects

Whereas the development of repositories for research content represents a relatively intuitive migration from pre-digital to post-digital research publishing practices, with same landmarks still visible (pre-prints, peer-review, journal titles and impact factors), when we move into the realm of teaching, we find a much less coherent transition taking place. The development of teaching material in digital form embraces both institutionally-authored material—lecture notes, image collections, animated programs, assessments as revision aids—and externally-published material (typically textbooks). Although it is conceivable that an institution could eventually capture all of its research outputs in an institutional repository, it is much less easy to see how its learning material could be captured so extensively. Copyright presents a major hurdle to this in itself, and institutions are not in such a strong position to seek copyright exemptions—even for textbooks to which they may have contributed—as they are with research papers written by their own academics.

In the same way, as applied to research outputs, learning object repositories can also be classified into disciplinary and institutional. In contrast to the situation with research materials, however, we find that institutional repositories of learning objects are relatively uncommon. It is rare as yet to find institutions which views the aggregated collection of their learning objects as having a useful 'showcase' value. In addition, Data Protection Act in the UK, and of the enquirer seeking access to corporate information for a valid reason (e.g. the Freedom of Information Act in the UK). Being digital, the assets themselves can be preserved, and can be interlinked in ways which make efficient use of both of them and of the time of staff maintaining or accessing them. This requires that a lifecycle approach to assets to be adopted by the institution, and at present, few institutions are doing this optimally.

Granular Content

Another challenge for the architects of systems based around repositories is presented by the granularity within objects. Documents are often compound objects, and so composed of more than a single file. A research paper may have colour photographs embedded within it, or an associated table of data. Learning objects, in particular, have a troublingly elastic definition. A learning object can be as large as a year-long course of study in a subject, or as small as a single image file. It is important that institutional repositories have the means to describe their objects both at the highest level of granularity—the document level—and at the lowest level for each constituent part which, for a variety of reasons, requires independent description.

Repository objects are, therefore, often hierarchies in themselves, sharing the character of archival records more than individual object catalogue records. Each constituent record of a document or object requires its own metadata and this has to show both the relationship of the part to the whole record, and also the rights which inhere in its referent. For example, a PhD thesis may include photographic images where the copyright is not owned by the author. The cataloguer of this thesis, then has to try to identify the rights ownership. This is not an easy task, and it is often solved for repository managers by devolving it to the authors themselves. Authors are clearly better placed to establish the copyright in embedded objects than cataloguers, and a workflow step to require this is regularly included.

What Role Do Institutional Repositories Play?

While institutional digital libraries are making inroads into the consciousness of their users, it is nevertheless true that the march of digital content via the web makes many of their services less vital than they were, and even redundant to a growing proportion of users on campus. The concept of institutionally is an increasingly fragile one when we consider digital content and digital libraries, and we, therefore, must ask whether we should be developing institutional repositories at all. Are they an attempt to shut the stable door after the horse has bolted? All institutional digital library services face a tough battle in being accepted on campuses because alternative systems usually exist, and their shortcomings are not always obvious. Institutional repositories are not an intuitively necessary development in the minds of most academics. Few people yet feel they do not need a physical library on their campus doorstep, but many—particularly those experienced in using subject-based repositories such as arXiv—are surprised to hear librarians arguing for the creation of institutional repositories as new services.

In pre-digital times, when researchers wrote up their results for publication, they would have been posted, hand-written or in typescript, to a publisher—the only agent with the technology to present the finished paper in a pleasing form, and to reproduce it in multiples sufficient to meet the likely demand across the world, in their journals.

Publishers also managed a third very important process—that of verification that the research was of a quality which made it valuable to other researchers. This is achieved by the system of peer review, and is critical to the advancement of knowledge, and, therefore, to the careers of researchers as they develop. If a piece of research is flawed or unoriginal, then the advancement of knowledge is stultified or even damaged, and at some future point this fact is likely to become obvious to other researchers, so that the researcher responsible is tarnished in the eyes of their peers—with obvious consequences for personal self-esteem and career development.

In the digital age, the presentation and reproduction functions do not require the intermediation of a publisher. This is what an institutional repository can do. In doing so, the institution is granted a capture function similar to the archival functions which have long existed—in pre-digital time also—for corporate records. Sending research papers to publishers immediately they have been written was a necessary process, but not an ideal one. If the overall work required is not made noticeably more arduous, how much better to record the outflow of the institution's research as it leaves the premises, stamping it at source with the institution's imprimatur and asserting ownership rights over it—either for the institution or for the author themselves. In the words of Herbert Van de Sompel, "Scholars deserve an innately digital scholarly communication system that is able to capture the digital scholarly record, make it accessible, and preserve it over time" (Van de Sompel et al., 2004). Van de Sompel's analysis is founded on a concern about data loss and the need to provide effective data curation, but it implies an emphasis on the role of the institution in the lifecycle nonetheless.

This new functionality is obviously desirable but was given little attention in the past because it was virtually impossible to administer, and there was no obvious benefit in any case. Institutional repositories now make the administration relatively simple, and the future benefits have come dramatically into focus in recent times. These benefits derive mainly from the extraordinary potential of repository networking which has been made possible through the development of the OAI-PMH protocol.

Herbert Van de Sompel, developer of OAI-PMH, has regularly described how the invention has the ability to serve the purposes of the academy—and the interested public—without sacrificing any of the tried and trusted elements of the research dissemination and publication process. He quotes the scholarly communication lifecycle model of Roosendal and Guertz, with its five key components (Roosendaal and Guertz, 1997):

> Registration: allows claims of precedence for a scholarly finding.
>
> Certification: establishes the validity of a registered scholarly claim.
>
> Awareness: allows actors in the scholarly system to remain aware of new claims and findings.
>
> Archiving: preserves the scholarly record over time.
>
> Rewarding: rewards actors for their performance in the communication system based on metrics derived from that system.

In the traditional print world, registration and certification require publishers, and awareness and archiving are carried out by libraries. Rewarding is done by a variety of actors, both institutional (e.g. promotion by the university) and at national and international levels, through rewards such as increased funding for research, visiting professorships, and invitations to contribute to scholarly works and conferences. In what Van de Sompel elsewhere describes as:

> This slow speed of response might be fatal for libraries. They may have the technology at an early stage, but they generally do not use it to engender change in their host institution's organisational practices, and so they run the risk of losing out to other players in the digital content marketplace. The greatest challenges of all for university libraries wishing to populate institutional repositories within their digital libraries may, therefore, be outreach and liaison. These are not activities which are normally given high priority, and this must change if libraries are to claim a key role in the scholarly communication lifecycle.

Metadata

There are two main components in the construction of digital libraries. One is technologies, several of which have been spawned by the digital library community itself. The other is metadata. Metadata has long been the 'bread and butter' of libraries. 'Data about data', as it is commonly described, metadata creation involves the production of records which act as proxies to the holdings of libraries, allowing those holdings to be discovered, whether the searcher is looking for a known item, or an item on a particular subject, or by a particular creator. For hundreds of years, cataloguing (still the favoured term by many librarians, rather than 'metadata creation' which can sound like an attempt to give a core library activity a pseudo-scientific digital age identity) was a local activity, designed to make usable the particular collections held by particular libraries in particular places. With the scale increase in volume of holdings typically held by libraries in the twentieth century, however, it soon became obvious that much of this labour could be shared so that the same items were not being separately catalogued in many different places. Subject indexing had already been standardised through the widespread adoption of the Dewey Decimal and Library of Congress schemes, among others, and cataloguing likewise became a standardised activity for an increasing proportion of the total, as libraries saw the benefits in sharing their efforts. Catalogue records, including standardised subject codes and headings, were initially posted out to subscribing libraries on cards, but were to become distributed over wide area networks from the early 1980s onwards, as the first generation of computer-based catalogues appeared in libraries.

The Machine Readable Cataloguing standard (MARC) evolved as an international standard, and is still massively used across the world for the cataloguing of books and journals according to a very detailed schema (defined set of record elements). MARC can be used for the description of items other than books and journals, but it falters in its capacity to describe the requirements of digital objects, and has been supplanted in digital repositories by other, more appropriate standards—none of which yet has the universality of use of MARC.

The document that one reads on a computer screen is assembled from a stack of machine protocols, a particular operating system, and applications software. The work may be stored in a single file, or be composed of several interrelated files. Each file will have a particular file format. Each of these components has a generation number. Besides that, an authoritative copy of the document may be stored in a digital store somewhere (or should be), and it will have a number of rights which exceed by some distance the relatively simple copyright with which the print world was familiar. There may be the separate rights of one or several creators, as well as the rights enjoyed by the reader of the document, and rights belonging to the institution which hosts the copy a reader may happen to be using. In short, for digital content, the description of the object —who created it, what it is called, what it is about, where it was published—is only one of the dimensions of metadata which need to be recorded in order for identification to take place.

The first generation of institutional repositories used the Qualified Dublin Core metadata schema to describe the content of their objects. Qualified Dublin Core is still widely used, mainly because it is specified by the OAI-PMH as a 'lowest common denominator' format well suited to supporting harvesting into a commonly structured repository, and, therefore, supporting discovery interoperability. Qualified Dublin Core utilises a 15-element record.

For learning objects, the IEEE Learning Object Metadata (LOM) standard tends to be used as the source schema. LOM implements the IMS Content Packaging standard, and so performs a similar task to METS in supporting the cataloguing of compound objects but within a pedagogical context.

The LOM standard, for example, has nine categories (General, Life cycle, Meta-Metadata, Technical, Educational, Rights, Relation, Annotation and Classification). Educational and Annotation are clearly categories which are quite specific to learning objects.

Cataloguing for the digital library requires skilled practitioners, and this may create a tension in libraries as traditional library catalogùing in the past few decades has increasingly been taken up by computer-based shared cataloguing systems which have reduced the burden of original cataloguing, and turned the bulk of print cataloguing activity into a relatively routine operation. By contrast, a metadata editor needs to know several different metadata schemas, and to apply them—or, often, to interpret them in a standardised way—to a heterogeneous range of digital object formats. The dominance of the age of MARC is over, when a single schema served for the description of any book or journal, and also for a few other things besides—realia (concrete objects housed in libraries, such as toys, or exhibition objects), and early websites among them. Now the metadata editor or creator has to be an artisan, with a variety of tools in their workshop, appropriate to the digital object in hand.

Repositories and Research Impact

Researchers are rewarded for their work not financially but through its impact. They want their research to be read, consumed and understood. They want their peers to comment on it, credit it and add to or extend it. Naturally, they want to receive credit for adding to human knowledge of the world; equally naturally, they want to help make the world a better place.

The conventional method of research dissemination via publication in journals is much more limited in its possible impact (through market forces) than the new method of publication of the same research in open access repositories. Studies have already shown that open access research papers are read more widely, and, therefore, cited more frequently, than papers which are not housed in repositories. The consequence of this is that they have greater impact.

The Institute of Scientific Information (ISI) has produced impact rankings for scholarly journals for many years, based upon its series of citation indexes, now web-based and known as Web of Knowledge (wok.mimas.ac.uk/). Impact factors are based upon the average number of times that papers in a given journal title are cited by other papers—a fair measure of their research impact, though not without some distortions, as ISI itself points out in its regular publication which presents impact rankings, the *Journal of Citation Reports*, where its online help text states: rather than individual papers. While a growing number of open access journal titles now exist, by which is meant that they are published free on the web with the costs of publication met by authors paying to publish, these are generally a poor measure of comparison because they are newly-founded journals competing against existing, established titles, and, therefore, almost inevitably producing less impact. Harnad and Brody point out this limitation, and suggest a way in which impact can be measured for papers deposited in open access repositories:

> To get a realistic estimate of the effect of OA on impact, it is not enough to compare only the 2% of ISI journals that are OA journals with the 98% that are not, to find that they are equal in impact (for this may well be comparing apples with oranges, even if you equate for subject matter). (Harnad and Brody, 2004)
>
> What further need to be compared is:
>
> - The citation impact of the much higher percentage (perhaps as high as 20-40% according to Swan and Brown's (2004) sample) of articles from the 98% non-OA journals that have been made OA by their authors (by self-archiving them) with
> - The citation impact of articles from those very same journals and issues that have not been made OA by their authors. (*Ibid.*)

Building on Steve Lawrence's seminal paper, 'Online or invisible' (Lawrence, 2001), Harnad and Brody's analysis of the physics literature for 2001 revealed that the ratio of open access article to non-open access article citations varied from 2.5:1 to 5.8:1. They are now extending the analysis to other disciplines. Kristin Antelman uses the same evidence in order to draw a significant conclusion for libraries. If they learn more about the working methods of the researchers in their institutions, they can provide a strong impetus to the adoption of open access repositories by researchers.

Antelman studied the relevant impact of open and restricted access papers in four disciplines—philosophy, political science, electronic and electrical engineering, and mathematics. She found that, while mathematics had the highest overall proportion of papers available on open access (69 per cent), the discipline in which the comparison between open and restricted access shows the greatest difference in impact measured by citations was in fact political science, which only had 29 per cent of its papers available on open access.

Scientists and social scientists are becoming more and more comfortable with reading articles in online form as a preference. The evidence from the arts and humanities does not yet bear this out, but Antelman believes that the behaviour of researchers in those fields will also change once a critical mass of papers is available in open access repositories. Lawrence points out the part that is played by convenience in the higher impact of open access papers. If papers are easy to get hold of, by being fully available from a usable online source, then they are more likely to be cited, particularly by researchers in a hurry. Libraries need to provide speedy access as part of their service (Ranganathan's Fourth Law), but they also observe a duty to ensure that the material they provide represents a balanced provision. It is ironic that one of the complaints made about some of the largest commercial publishers is that they have manipulated the convenience factor in order to serve their own commercial advantage, by putting their own journal articles within such easy reach of academics that they can benefit from the growing profile of their own titles whose impact factors are thereby boosted. Jean-Claude Guédon points this out in his seminal 2002 work In Oldenburg's Long Shadow: Librarians, Research Scientists, Publishers, and the Control of Scientific Publishing:

> If, through the manipulation of the number of articles in a given database, a publisher manages to affect the rate of use of its own articles, it also stands to reason that this publisher is able to affect the citation rate of its articles.

What holds true for a commercial publisher with a vast number of full-text articles available to subscribing institutions could equally hold true for a large, interoperating, worldwide network of open access full-text institutional repositories. As Antelman remarks, the comprehensiveness of this network is likely to have a beneficial consequence for the quality of research.

Conclusion

A growing proportion of the research community has discovered the utility of the web for the dissemination of their research outputs, and has now been using it—for many years in the case of some disciplines. The approach has been somewhat haphazard, however, as scholars are neither publishers nor librarians. The library community, increasingly focused on a digital library agenda, has understood the need to intervene in order to ensure that the material being disseminated is managed successfully through proper description, indexing and storage for long-term preservation. The approach which has now proved its value and begun to gain ground for research outputs is also now being used for other types of material which are generated within institutions.

The marriage of research generation by academics, with output management by librarians, has created a new form of publication, with open values, which presents a growing challenge to the commercial publishers which have controlled research publication for many decades. Commercial publishers operate on the assumption of a profit motive both for themselves and for their authors. As this motive is absent in the case of academics seeking the publication of their research, it may be that with this new form of publication in repositories owned and run from within the academy, research publication has finally found its most appropriate form.

References

American Council of Learned Societies 2006. Our Cultural Commonwealth: The report of the American Council of Learned Societies Commission on Cyber infrastructure for the Humanities and Social Sciences. Retrieved April 4, 2008 from http://www.acls.org/programs/Default.aspx?id=644

Ashworth, S. 2006. Role of Librarians in the Development of Institutional Repositories Retrieved on March 15, 2008 from http://www.pfsl.poznan.pl/oa/ppt/2.ppt

Barton, M.R. and Waters, M.M. 2004. Creating an Institutional Repository: LEADIRS Workbook. MIT Libraries. Retrieved April 6, 2008 from http://www.dspace.org/implement/leadirs.pdf

Candee, C. 2006. Changing the paradigm, An Interview. Retrieved May 1, 2008 from http://poynder.blogspot.com/2006/01/changing-paradigm.html

Chan, D.L.H., Kwok, C.S.Y. and Yip, S.K.F. 2005. Changing roles of reference librarians: The case of the HKUST Institutional Repository. Reference Services Review, 33(3), 268-82, Retrieved on March 15th 2008 from http://repository.ust.hk/dspace/bitstream/1783.1/2039/2/p268.pdf

Crow, R. 2002. The Case for Institutional Repositories: A SPARC Position Paper, Retrieved April 26, 2008 from http://www.arl.org/sparc/bm~doc/ir_final_release_102.pdf

DSpace Project. 2000. MIT Faculty Newsletter, XII (4), Retrieved April 27, 2008 from http://www.dspace.org//news/articles/dspace-project.html

ePrints website FAQ (n.d.). What is the purpose of self-archiving? What is the Open Archives Initiative (OAI)? Self-archiving FAQ. Retrieved April 24, 2008 from http://www.eprints.org/openaccess/self-faq/

For definitions, see MPEG-21. 2003. 'Information Technology, Multimedia Framework, Part 2: Digital Item Declaration', ISO/IEC 21000-2:2003; 2. Advanced Distributed Learning (2003) 'The Sharable Content Object Reference Model (SCORM) – Version 1.3 – WD'.

Gibbons, S. 2004. Benefits of an institutional repository. *Library Technology Reports*, 40(4), 11-16.

Hunter, D. 2007. Repository: Publication or archive? JISC_Repositories listserve discussion thread, Retrieved April 6, 2008 from www.jiscmail.ac.uk/archives/jisc-repositories.html

Johnson, R. 2002. Institutional repositories: Partnering with faculty to enhance scholarly communication. *D-Lib Magazine*, 8(11), retrieved May 8th from http://www.dlib.org/dlib/november02/johnson/11johnson.html

Lynch, C. 2003. Institutional Repositories: Essential Infrastructure for Scholarship in the Digital Age. ARL, 226, Retrieved April 13, 2008 from http://www.arl.org/bm~doc/br226ir.pdf

Markey et al. 2007. Census of Institutional Repositories in the United States. Retrieved April 6, 2008 from http://www.google.co.bw/h?hl=en&q=Markey+2007+Council+on+Library+and+Information+Resour ces+%2B+institutional+repository&btnG=Search&meta

Markey, K. Rieh, S.Y., St. Jean, B., Kim, J., and Yakel, E. (2007, February). Census of Institutional Repositories in the United

States: MIRACLE Project Research Findings. Washington, D.C.: Council on Library and Information Resources. Available: http://www.clir.org/pubs/reports/pub140/pub140.pdf

Rusbridge, C., Burnhill, P., Ross, S., Buneman, P., Giaretta, D., Lyon, L., and Atkinson, M. 2005. The Digital Curation Centre: A Vision for Digital Curation. From Local to Global Data Interoperability—Challenges and Technologies. Mass Storage and Systems Technology Committee of the IEEE Computer Society. June 20-24, 2005. Sardinia, Italy. Available: http://www.dcc.ac.uk/docs/DCC_Sardinia_paper_final.pdf

Yeates, R. 2003. Over the Horizon: Institutional Repositories. VINE: *The Journal of Information and Knowledge Management Systems*, 33(2), 96-99.

14

Trends and Development of Institutional Repositories (IRs) in India

Krishna Kumar Kesharwani and Jai Prakash Singh

ABSTRACT

The institutional repositories are digital collections that capture and preserve the intellectual output of university communities, respond to various strategic issues facing academic institutions. This chapter discusses the concept of Institutional Repository (IR), its relevance, merits, software requirements and the current trends in India.

Keywords: *Academic Institution; Software; Digital Scholarship; Institutional Repository; Librarians; Authors; Contributors and Users in IR.*

Introduction

An Institutional Repository (IR) is a digital archive where a university community's intellectual work is made accessible and preserved for posterity. The concept of IR suggests the tantalizing possibility of greater library influence over the full cycle of scholarly communication on campus, from research through publication, collection, and preservation. Libraries are performing lead role in shaping institutional digital repositories all over the world. According to Clifford Lynch "a university-based institutional repository is a set of services that a university offers to the members of its community for the management and dissemination of digital materials created by the institution and its community members. It is most essentially an organizational commitment to the stewardship of these digital materials, including long-term preservation where appropriate, as well as organization and access or distribution" (1).

Institutional Repositories: Need and Objectives

The rhetoric about open access is that the presentation of the institution's published research output via a repository would inevitably improve its visibility and raise the profile of both the institution and the researchers involved, and it would potentially lead to greater citation frequency and impact of the published items (Robinson, 2009). The main reasons for establishing an IR given by a sample of ARL libraries surveyed was "to increase the global visibility to preserve and provide free access and to collect and organize the institution's scholarship".

The four main objectives for having an IR are to:

- (i) create global visibility for an institution's scholarly research;
- (ii) collect content at a single location;
- (iii) provide open access to institutional research output by self-archiving it; and
- (iv) store and preserve other institutional digital assets, including unpublished otherwise easily lost ("Grey") literature (e.g., theses or technical reports). (Gopikuttan, 2008)

An institutional repository is not a substitute for the traditional publishing process that leads to tenure and promotion, but it can operate tangentially with those practices in building up a scholar's recognition (Gaffney, 2008, 574). Immediate unrestricted access to scientific ideas, methods, results and conclusions will speed up the progress of science, technology and medicine and will more directly bring the benefits of research to the public (Nazim and Maya Devi, 2008). Institutional repositories have the potential to bring together intellectual output of the researchers of the institution and make it available and accessible to the public through Internet. While faculty publications reflect positively on the host university, the interoperable repositories demonstrate the reputation and quality of the institution, and the scientific, social and economic relevance of its research output. Institutional repositories help to measure the productivity of the institution and increase the institution's visibility, prestige, status and public value. At individual level, a strong institutional repository enhances the visibility of the communities and helps to identify the expertise of the communities belonging to it. It also helps publications in receiving more citations by the fellow scholars due to its free access facility without geographical boundary. It also helps in establishing priorities for their research findings (made possible by data sampling and publication identifier); share unpublished ideas with peers and obtain feedback; and support long-term preservation of their research output.

1. Relevance of Institutional Repository

The building of an Institutional Repository for any organization is needed in the present scenario of digital world because of the following certain changes:

(i) Technological changes;

(ii) Significant increase in the overall volume of research;

(iii) Increasing need of archival and access to unpublished information bearing objects; and

(iv) Increasing demand to access knowledge objects from anywhere at any-time.

Increasing uncertainty over who will handle the preservation archiving of digital scholarly research materials.

2. The Importance of the Standard IR Project

(i) It will help to develop a national research repository infrastructure by setting up, populating and linking individual repositories;

(ii) It will stimulate development of services that draws research information made available through the repository infrastructure;

(iii) It will provide a window that gives open access to improve the sponsoring institution's visibility and status; and

(iv) It will support the open-access model of publication.

3. Benefits of Institutional Repository

(a) For the Contributor:

(i) **Greater citation:** Studies have shown that articles freely available on the Internet are cited more often than their paper counterparts.

(ii) **Speed:** Faculty members can self-publish their pre-prints immediately, with the possibility of receiving immediate feedback.

(iii) **Organization:** An institutional repository can contain all of the scholarly work by one faculty member, including material such as pre-prints, post-prints, presentations, and classroom materials (dependent on copyright restrictions). Instead of being scattered about in different databases, servers, or computer hard drives, this material can be browsed easily in one place by the user, and reused easily by the contributor.

(iv) **Preservation:** In order to ensure continued access, digital files need to be refreshed and migrated. Ten years from now, will you be able to open a Microsoft Word file you've created today? Depositing a file into an institutional repository means that the burden of ensuring the file can be opened is placed on the curator of the institutional repository, and not on the owner.

(v) **Ease of use:** Although self-submission is possible in our institutional repository, it's much more likely that all uploading will be done by the library. All that is needed are files to upload and permission to upload it.

(vi) **Permanent place:** Depositing an item into an institutional repository means that it stays in one place and maintains the same URL.

(b) For the Institution:

(i) The scholarly material produced by the university is available in one place, reflecting the intellectual achievements of the institution, and serving as a valuable marketing tool.

(ii) Documents reflecting the institutional history of the university, both scholarly and non-scholarly, are preserved for future use, much like a traditional archive preserves paper material.

(iii) Material that is not traditionally published is included in the repository, including drafts of unpublished articles or book chapters, unpublished research, student works, learning objects, and creative works.

(c) For the User:

(i) Material in an institutional repository can be found through a search engine.

(ii) There is no charge to access this material, and there are no subscription fees. Our repository contains material that is best displayed in its original digital format, such as audio files, video files, animations, and data sets.

(iii) Gray literature, material not easily found through conventional means, will be actively recruited for the repository. This can include material such as working papers, pre-prints, white papers, conference presentations.

Other Benefits

(i) Increased visibility to the Library;

(ii) Complete customization of policies and user interface;

(iii) Responsiveness to local user needs and preferences;

(iv) Increased contact with constituents;

(v) Showcase and preserve scholarly output and historic documents;

(vi) Archive post-prints, pre-prints (and extra materials);

(vii) Support teaching and learning;

(viii) Provide curatorial stewardship for disorganized and scattered digital materials;

(ix) Papers will get persistent URL and more citations; and

(x) No need of maintaining server or back up.

Trends and Development of Information Repositories (IRs) in India

A few of India's premier institutions, particularly in the science and technology area, are providing open access to their research publications. In these repositories, access to retrospective material appears to be substantial; both in terms of research articles and theses with less access to pre-prints and current publications. Much of the content is designed to showcase the intellectual product of the institution giving wide coverage to publications in international journals and less of the "hidden science" targeted by open access advocates (Fernandez, 2006). In India, the efforts towards adopting open access initiative have already been started. But there are some hurdles and misunderstandings about open access among the Indian research community. These are: lack of expertise in every organization to promote creation of institutional archives and encourage scientists to place their papers in them; lack of infrastructural facilities like hardware and connectivity of high bandwidth; Scientists are under the impression that the editors of renowned journals may not accept the archived papers. Scientists are not aware of the fact that the attitudes of the journals are now changing and renowned journals also now permit the authors to archive both pre-prints and post-prints (Hirwade and Hirwade, 2006).

In India, poor access to international journals and the low visibility of papers are major problems being faced by Indian researchers. Open access is viewed as a solution to this deficit (Fernandez, 2006). Development of IRs in Indian Universities and R&D Organizations is a growing phenomenon, with an increasing number of libraries planning to implement it. In India, the process of growth of IRs or to have a strong platform for the development of IRs is encouraging with the significant proliferation of open access and digital library initiatives.

The development of IRs in universities and R&D organizations helps in managing and sharing research resources among the scholarly community. Universities in India can also make their research publications more visible and accessible by encouraging their researchers to deposit their scholarly publications into the institutional repository. With the development of Information and Communication Technologies (ICT), the concept of IR is gaining momentum today not only in developed but also in developing countries including India. In recent years, Open Access is becoming a movement in India and a large number of organizations are taking initiative for this. University Grants Commission (UGC), All India Council of Technical Education (AICTE), Council of Scientific and Industrial Research (CSIR) and National Knowledge Commission (NKC) of Govt. of India are also providing help and support for the development of infrastructure and other related matters for sustainable development of IRs in Indian universities. University Grants Commission (UGC) provides grants placed at its disposal by the Central Government to universities established by Central and State Governments for various research projects and activities.

UGC through Information and Library Network (INFLIBNET) has been serving towards modernization of libraries through a National Network of libraries in around 264 universities, colleges and R&D institutions across the country. The OAI repository of INFLIBNET, which is named as "Shodhganga" is developed with DSpace open source software which collects, preserves and disseminates the post-prints, pre-prints, news clippings, CALIBER and PLANNER full text proceedings, training material and other scholarly publications of it. UGC has developed a policy document on building university level Institutional Digital Repository, which aims to improve the local access to global research and global access to local research. UGC through its national policy framework (2005) proposed and made it mandatory for all the researchers of Indian universities to submit their Doctoral theses, dissertations in electronic form for the creation of Indian National Theses Database to ensure free access to research theses. Through INFLIBNET, UGC is also taking initiatives to develop the ICT infrastructure and support in all the universities run under its purview.

Usage of Open Access Repository Software in India

Name of the Software	Total No. of the User
DSpace	87
E-Prints	46
GSDL	26

Conclusion

Institutional repositories enhance teaching, learning, and research and are considered as a boon to the scholarly community. Institutional repositories have a great potential for improving visibility and impact of institutional research. The establishment of IRs in a developing country like India will help to get access to global research results, and in turn global presence to the local research results. The Indian researchers, library and information professionals, administrators of Academic and R&D institutions must be aware of the new opportunities provided by information and communication technologies and the advantages of IRs. The awareness programs, training and workshops, funded by the leading organizations like UGC, CSIR, etc., to educate and instruct the faculty members, researchers and scientists and all other working bodies to adopt the "open access" approach must be more widespread. They must be encouraged to self-archive their research outputs in institutional repositories. Though, most of the universities in India are lacking in infrastructure for establishing institutional repositories but today with the availability of several free, open source repository software packages it has become relatively easy to establish IRs. So, all the universities, R&D institutions in India which are being run by public or private fund should also establish their own repositories to make their research widely accessible by scholarly community throughout the world and to ensure its long-term preservation for future use. Moreover, to enhance the visibility of the established institutional repositories, they must be registered with open access registries such as ROAR, OpenDOAR and federated search services such as OAIster.

References

Crow, R. 2002. The case for institutional repositories: A SPARC position paper. The Scholarly Publishing and Academic Resources Coalition, Washington, DC. Retrieved March 15, 2011 from http://www.arl.org/sparc/bm~doc/ir_final_release_102.pdf

Fernandez, L. 2006. Opens access initiatives in India: An evaluation. *Partnership: The Canadian Journal of Library and Information Practice and Research,* 1(1), 1-22. Retrieved May 8, 2011 from http://journal.lib.uoguelph.ca/index.php/perj/article/viewFile/110/172

Gaffney, M. 2008. Involving the library and campus community in institutional repository projects. *The Serials Librarian*, 55(4), 568-76. doi:10.1080/03615260802380411

Gopikuttan, A. 2008. Current developments in library and information services. *Journal of Information Science and Technology,* 1(1), 89-100.

Hirwade, M. and Hirwade, A. 2006. Institutional repositories: Challenge and opportunity for LIS Professionals in digital age. *Library Herald*, 44(2), 146-51. Retrieved May 3, 2011 from http://eprints.rclis.org/bitstream/10760/7987/1/7D311B68.pdf

Lynch, C.A. 2003. Institutional repositories: Essential infrastructure for scholarship in the digital age. ARL: A Bimonthly Report on Research Library Issues and Actions from ARL, CNI, and SPARC, no. 226, 1-7. Retrieved January 18, 2011 from http://www.arl.org/bm~doc/br226ir.pdf

Nazim, M. and Maya Devi. 2008. Open access journals and institutional repositories: Practical need and present trends in India. *Annals of Library and Information Studies*, 55, 27-34. Retrieved May 8, 2011 from http://nopr.niscair.res.in/bitstream/123456789/825/1/ALIS%2055%281%29%20%282008 %29%2027-34.PDF

Poornima, N., Biradar, B.S. and Goudar, I.R.N. 2008. Enhancing the impact of Indian scholarly communication through institutional repositories. ILA Platinum Jubilee International Conference on quote; Knowledge for all: Role of libraries and information centers quote, 12-15 November, Mumbai, India. Retrieved May 10, 2011 from http://nal-ir.nal.res.in/4924/1/poornima.docx

Robinson, M. 2009. Promoting the visibility of educational research through an institutional repository. *Serials Review*, 35(3), 133-37. Retrieved May 3, 2011 from http://libir1.ied.edu.hk/pubdata/ir/link/pub/Robinson_IR_Paper_Final.pdf

15

Institutional Repositories in Indian Higher Education

D.B. Shinde

ABSTRACT

The chapter deals with the concept of Institutional Repositories and their benefits to the institutions. The role of IRs in Higher Education has also been discussed in the chapter. It also discusses those digital repository contents that needs to be preserved and disseminated.

Keywords: *Institutional Repository; Open Source Software; Digital Content; DSpace; ICT.*

Introduction

Nowadays, traditional academic libraries are moving forward to adopt the Information Communication Technology tools and techniques to provide digital information globally. India has the second largest educational system in the world. A focus on quality, access and relevance of higher education to achieve the required social transformation for sustainable economic development of the country has been the national priority. Government of India has provided huge amount of funds for education and research. The universities are generating a large amount of information resources in digital form. Institutional Repositories became popular and powerful tool that permit institutions to store, maintain and share their digital collection. The University Grant Commission (UGC) has to take initiatives to build up Institutional Repositories at higher education level to provide the quality of information, the services. Now, institutions have started to build up their own digital repositories. For setup

Institutional Repositories, the open access Repository Softwares are available on non-profit basis under open source licenses to build Institutional Repositories and support digital archive and institutions.

What is an Institutional Repository?

The term of Institutional Repository is a collection of digital documents of the intellectual product generated by the authors, researchers and students of the Institution and accessible for students and the community nationally and internationally.

An institutional repository is an online archive for collecting, preserving, and disseminating digital copies of the intellectual output of an institution, particularly a research institution. The development of an IR redefines the production and dissemination of scholarly material within an academic community (Wikipedia).

Clifford Lynch (2003) defined an Institutional repository as an organization based set of services which the organization offers to the members of its community for the management and dissemination of digital materials created by the institution and its community members. It is most essentially an organizational commitment to the stewardship of these digital materials, including long-term preservation, where appropriate, as well as organization and access or distribution.

The Institutional Repository can be created on his own with their policy. The Institutional Repository can be useful for different contents i.e. Doctoral theses, pre-print and post-prints of papers. And can also add other contents of Institutional and learning objects such as journals of institution, Rules and Regulations, technical reports, video recording, Audio and Video material, Class notes, Bibliography on full text, Presentations, Blogs, etc.

The Purpose of Institutional Repositories

The institutions of higher education all over the world are experiencing the necessity of managing their education, research and resources in a more effective and open way. By making the research and scientific output easily available, they will support the development of new relationships between the academicians and both national and international research centres. This will facilitate the institutions of the higher education so that they will have to realise that learning improvement is the key for the success of the information society.

Characteristics

The following characteristics of Institutional Repository are:

1. It is institutionally defined—unlike a subject repository: the IR captures only the intellectual output of host institution.
2. Content may be partly scholarly or may comprise administrative teaching and research materials, both published and unpublished.
3. It is cumulative and perpetual. Once items are submitted they should not be withdrawn. This carries with it a long-term obligation on the host institution to preserve Institutional Repository content.
4. In collecting, storing and disseminating information it contributes to the process of scholarly communication.

Institutional Repositories Contents

There are varieties of documents in electronic form which can be stored in the Institutional Repositories for the future research and also used as teaching aids for the teachers and student. An Institutional Repository captures, preserves, disseminates information and provides access to the intellectual output of an institution. Some contents are categorized as follows:

Scientific Objects

- Doctoral thesis in the public domain
- Doctoral theses read in the institution
- Communications at congresses, posts, posters
- Pre-prints and post-prints of papers published in journals
- Audio/Video visual materials
- Journals of the institution
- Patents
- Datasets
- Software

1. Institutional Objects

- Institutional information journals
- Rules and Regulations
- Archive documents
- Posts, poster, work documents, technical reports.

2. Learning Objects

- Study and exercise materials
- Class notes
- Simulators
- Bibliography
- Presentation
- Online tests
- Laboratory guides.

Advantages of IR

A repository has the following purposes and benefits for an institution:

- Opens up the outputs of the university to the world.
- Maximizes the visibility and impact of these outputs as a result.
- Showcases the university to interested constituencies—prospective staff, prospective students and other stakeholders.
- Collects and curates digital outputs.
- Manages and measures research and teaching activities.
- Provides a workspace for work-in-progress, and for collaborative or large-scale projects.
- Enables and encourages interdisciplinary approaches to research.
- Facilitates the development and sharing of digital teaching materials and aids.
- Supports student endeavours, providing access to thesis and dissertations and a location for the development of e-portfolios.

Why IRs in Higher Education?

Institutional repositories are a new but important method for capturing, collecting, managing, disseminating and preserving scholarly works created in digital form within the educational landscape. Institutional repositories are a practical, cost effective and statistic means for academic institutions for building partnerships with their faculty to advance scholarly communication. The Universities and Academic Institutions are generating huge amount of information resources day by day in international publications. Apart from teachers, research students are also generating various information resources as primary sources i.e., Scientific, Institutional and Learning objects. They are implementing institutional repositories which rests on two interrelated propositions—one that supports a broad, pan-institutional effort and another, that offers direct and immediate benefits to each institution, authors, users and Library and Information Centres. Institutional repository facilitates long-term preservation through centralized planning and support. National Assessment and Accreditation Council (NAAC), Bengaluru is promoting and adopting best practices in large academic institutional libraries.

Institutional Repositories Softwares

There are varieties of open source software packages [DSpace (MIT) and EPrints (Southampton) and Fedora as well as Greenstone] are available on non-profit basis under open source licenses to build Institutional Repositories and support digital archive.

- Open Source Softwares (Table 1).
- Some Commercial Digital Repository Softwares.
- Apart from the above Open Source Softwares, some commercially developed softwares are also available for digital repository. The name of few is mentioned herein (Table 2).
- CONTENTdm®: Developed at the University of Washington and distributed by OCLC. The software has tools for acquiring or creating collections; tools for storage of the content and a set of tools for display and retrieval of objects.

Table 1
List of Latest Released Versions of Open Source Softwares

Sl. No.	Softwares	URL	Developer	Operating System	Version
1.	Dspace	http://www.dspace.org/	MIT Libraries & HP Labs	Linux, Solaris, Unix, Ubuntu and Windows	DSpace 6.x, released Oct. 24, 2016
2.	Eprints	http://www.eprints.org/uk/	University of Southampton	Linux, Solaris, Unix, Ubuntu, Mac OS and Windows	V3.4 released June 14, 2016
3.	Fedora	https://getfedora.org/	DuraSpace	Linux, Mac OS and Windows	GNOME 3.22 released Nov. 22, 2016
4.	MyCore	http://www.mycore.org/	MyCore Team	Linux, Solaris, Unix, or Windows	V2016.16, released June 27, 2016
5.	Invenio	http://invenio-software.org/	CERN Document Server Software Consortium	Unix , Windows	V2.1.1, released Sep. 1, 2015
6.	Opus	http://www.kobv.de/entwicklung/software/opus-4/	Cooperative Library Network of Berlin-Brandenburg (KOBV)	Linux and Windows	V21:42, released April 3, 2015
7.	SobekCM	http://sobekrepository.org/	Mark V. Sullivan	Window	V4.10.1 released Dec. 23, 2016
8.	Greenstone	http://www.greenstone.org/	University of Waikato	Linux, Unix and Windows	V3.08 released Nov. 23, 2016

- Digi Tool: This is an enterprise solution for the management of digital assets in libraries and academic environment.
- EN Compass: It is a one module of EN Compass or suite of software for managing and accessing digital content. EN Compass has many modules for various purposes.
- Hyperion: It provides organization, storage and access to digital files by searching both associated Metadata and full text of text files.
- Meta Source: Meta source is a suite of tools used to manage digital collections, including, digital object storage, crawling external collections and support for Metadata schemes.
- VITAL: VITAL is an institutional repository software developed by VTLS. VITAL is a set of workflow extensions, management utilities and enhanced searching capabilities build on Fedora Repository Architecture.

Institutional Repository in India

In India, the University Grant Commission (UGC) has to take initiative to build up Institutional Repositories at higher education level and release Regulation 2005 for submission of digital object in electronic format so that, it can easily be made available to community. India is the second largest country in which number of Academic, Research, Government, Corporate Institutions are using open access digital repository. Some of them institutions setup and designed their own institutional repositories with valuable information sources and services. DSpace is the popular and largest user in the world; 22016 institutions are using Institutional Repository Software, while in India 163 Academic, Government and Research Institutions are using it.

Table 2
List of Institutional Repository setup in India

Sl. No.	Name of the Instituion	Place	URL	No. of Items	Software
1	Mysore University	Mysore	http://eprints.uni-mysore.ac.in/	NA	Eprints
2	INFLIBNET	Ahmedabad	http://ir.inflibnet.ac.in/	1589	Dspace
3	Goa University	Goa	http://irgu.unigoa.ac.in/drs/	4631	Dspace
4	Tezpur University	Tezpur	http://agnee.tezu.ernet.in:8082/jspui/	307	Dspace
5	Pondicherry University	Puducherry	http://dspace.pondiuni.edu.in/jspui/	789	Dspace
6	North Eastern Hill University	Shillong	http://dspace.nehu.ac.in/	9764	Dspace
7	IIT-BOMBAY	Bombay	http://dspace.library.iitb.ac.in/jspui/	18108	Dspace
8	IIT-DELHI	Delhi	http://eprint.iitd.ac.in/	6284	Dspace
9	IIT-Gandhi Nagar	Gandhi Nagar	http://repository.iitgn.ac.in/	1766	Dspace
10	IIT-GUWAHATI	Guwahati	http://gyan.iitg.ernet.in/	678	Dspace
11	IIT-HYDRABAD	Hydrabad	http://raiith.iith.ac.in/	2761	Eprints
12	IIT-ROORKI	Roorki	http://roar.eprints.org/5420/	NA	Dspace
13	IIM-AHMEDABAD	Ahmedabad	http://vslir.iima.ac.in/xmlui/	17259	Dspace
14	IIM-BENGALURU	Bengaluru	http://research.iimb.ernet.in/	3991	Dspace
15	IIM-KOZHIKODE	Kozhikode	http://dspace.iimk.ac.in/	744	Dspace

Role of the Library in Building IR

Considering the increased benefits of institutional repositories, it is conceivable that establishing IR will be the next significant movement in the library landscape. As a result, the libraries will have many roles to play to build up successful IRs.

Libraries have always been engaged in managing their institutional collections, accumulating abundant expertise in collection assessment, organization and development. The libraries have a key role to play in building IRs. Library roles are becoming more deeply engaged with the broader vision of the institution by being more intertwined and interdependent with other stakeholders, such as the university administration, faculty, and other departments. Most of the faculty do not have the time to stay abreast of changes in information technology and will consider self-archiving as extra administrative work. Lougee describes this role as diffuse, meaning libraries are becoming a more integrated part of the community by infusing library expertise into research, teaching, learning, and service functions. The library's level of relevance and visibility to faculty and the institution will increase as librarians support faculty in their digital publishing activities. He further states that libraries can involve in developing IRs and serve as a collaborator in research, teaching and learning.

- Educate faculty on the importance of open access for global sharing of scholarship with enhanced professional visibility for the author and the institution.
- Negotiating with publishers on behalf of faculty or encouraging faculty to retain the right to publish in IRs as well as in scholarly publications.
- Depositing materials in IRs on behalf of researchers and undertaking file formatting and conversion.
- IRs allow libraries to provide direct access to scholarly materials instead of through the systems of serials' publishers and vendors.
- The biggest challenge of the IR appears to be generating contents for it. Libraries should take necessary steps for promoting IR resources. The librarians have to become marketing specialists to popularize IR.
- According to The Scholarly Publishing and Academic Resources Coalition (SPARC), managing and

participating in evolving scholarly communication process is a new challenge for libraries. Committing to an institutional repository requires libraries to carefully consider the implications of moving beyond a custodial role model to actively contributing to the evolution of scholarly communication, a paradigm shift from the traditional role to a more practical and enriched institutional landscape. (Crow, 2002)

Conclusion

Digital repository becomes powerful tool to facilitate capturing, preserving, accessing and retrieving the intellectual information materials to access globally. Govt. of India, HRD-UGC realizes the importance and has taken initiatives to setup institutional repository at higher educational level. In India, number of academic and research institution like IITs, IIMs, Central Universities, State Universities, INFLIBNET, CSIR has created their own institutional repositories by using DSpace, EPrints, Greenstone mostly. These are available through non-profit open source licenses software. DSpace is the popular repository software internationally, and numbers of institutions have taken steps to develop their own institutional repository.

References

Alan, McCord. 2003. Institutional Repositories: Enhancing Teaching, Learning, and Research. 1-7 pp. accessed https://net.educause.edu/ir/library/pdf/DEC0303.pdf dated 19 Jan 2017.

Ashok Kumar, N. Institutional Repositories in India. accessed https://core.ac.uk/download/pdf/11889645.pdf dated 25 January 2017.

Chakraborty, Susmita and Ghosh, S.B. Open Resources for Higher Education: The Indian Scenario. 1-10pp. accessed http://www.bg.pw.edu.pl/ iatul2011/proceedings /ft/ Chakraborty_S.pdf dated 19 January 2017.

Clifford A. Lynch. 2003. Institutional Repositories: Essential Infrastructure for Scholarship In The Digital Age. Libraries and the Academy 3.2. 327-36pp. accessed https://muse.jhu.edu/article/42865/summary dated 27 January 2017.

Ellen, Finnie Duranceau and Sue, Kriegsman. Implementing Open Access Policies Using Institutional Repositories. 75-97pp. accessed http://www.ala.org/alcts/sites/ala.org.alcts/files/content/resources/papers/ir_ch05_.pdf dated 21 January 2017.

http://eprints.rclis.org/13512/2/Guidelines_IR_english.pdf dated 19 January 2017.

http://ir.inflibnet.ac.in/bitstream/1944/1747/1/IR%20Using%20DSpace.pdf dated 19 January 2017.

http://shodhganga.inflibnet.ac.in/simple-search?query=institutional+repository&go= accessed 22 January 2017.

http://www.duraspace.org/registry/dspace dated 25 January 2017.

http://www.naac.gov.in/docs/Students%20Participation%20in%20Quality%20Enhancement.pdf dated 26 January 2017.

http://www.openscholarship.org/upload/docs/application/pdf/200909/open_access_institutional_repositories.pdf dated 21 January 2017.

http://www.unesco.org/new/fileadmin/MULTIMEDIA/HQ/CI/CI/pdf/news/institutional_repository_software.pdf dated 19 January 2017.

https://blogs.libraries.indiana.edu/scholcomm/2011/08/23/2-what-is-an-institutional-repository/dated 21 January 2017.

https://en.wikipedia.org/wiki/Institutional_repository dated 24 January 2017.

Kanchan, Kamila. 2009. Institutional Repository Projects in India. 7th International CALIBER. 128-32pp. accessed http://www.inflibnet.ac.in/caliber2009/CaliberPDF/17.pdf dated 23 January 2017.

Karmarkar, Gouri Sankar, Das, Rumi and Thakuria, Juli. 2010. Institutional Repositories in India: A Comparative Study of Dspace and Eprints. 7th Convention PLANNER 423-34pp. accessed http://ir.inflibnet.ac.in/bitstream/1944/983/1/43.pdf dated 19 January 2017.

Lucy, A. Tedd. 2009. Open Access Publishing and Institutional Repositories: An Overview. 7th International CALIBER. 572-82pp. accessed http://www.inflibnet.ac.in/caliber2009/CaliberPDF/71.pdf dated 23 January 2017.

Tabasum, Hashim and Tariq, Rashid Jan. (2011). Institutional Repositories: An Evaluative Study. TRIM 7(2) July-Dec 2011. 229-36pp. accessed http://www.inflibnet.ac.in/ojs/index.php/TRIM/article/view/1257/1138 dated 21 January 2017.

Tansley, Rober et al. 2003. The DSpace Institutional Digital Repository System: Current Functionality. Proceedings of Joint Conference on Digital Libraries. Accessed https://pdfs.semanticscholar.org/7b37/db48f14bc22336a3409f294c2cf4a1735aaa.pdf dated 19 January 2017.

Thakuria, Juli. 2008. Building an Institutional Repository with Dspace. Planner 102-14pp. accessed https://dspace3-labs.atmire.com/bitstream/handle/123456789/22917/Dspace%20paper.pdf?sequence=1 dated 19 January 2017.

Vishala, B.K. and Bhandi, M.K. 2007. Building Institutional Repository (IR): Role of the Library. 5th International CALIBER. 631-40pp. accessed http://ir.inflibnet.ac.in/bitstream/1944/1438/1/631-640.pdf dated 21 January 2017.

16

Study of Library and Information Science Theses on Shodhganga Repositories

Vyas Jagdish R.

ABSTRACT

The present chapter has attempted to overview the current status of E-theses repositories in India. The UGC Notification (Minimum Standards and Procedure for Award of M.Phil./Ph.D Degree, Regulation, 2016) dated May 5, 2016 mandates submission of electronic version of theses and dissertations by the researchers in universities with an aim to facilitate open access to Indian theses and dissertations to the academic community world-wide. Electronic theses in Library and Information Science subject submitted by different Universities on Shodhganga upto December 5, 2016 will be studied in present chapter. There were 843 e-theses submitted by 66 universities on Shodhganga.

Keywords: *Shodhganga; Repository; ETD; Theses Academic Community Electronic these and dissertations.*

Introduction

Research is a most important intellectual activity in the higher education system which provides dependable solutions to the problems being manifested in various fields of knowledge. Research brings prestige not only to the nation and the department/university but also to the research scholar. Today in this competitive world, no university can afford to remain static, it has to evolve continually and consciously by adding new ideas, inventions and discoveries in different fields of knowledge through research. Research generates new knowledge which ensures development of a subject, and helps to establish sound theories of the subject. Research is directly responsible for the social and economic development of a country. Research in Library Science dates back to 1950s when Manindra Nath Basu was awarded Ph.D on a topic, 'Museum methods and the process of cleaning and preservation' from University of Calcutta.

Earlier, researchers were not able to access all the scholarly literature published across the world due to lack of proper communication technologies. With the advent of Information and Communication Technology (ICT), this problem is solved to a major extent and the results of the research going throughout the world made available to the public without any restriction. The researchers adopted Budapest Open Access Initiative (BOAI) in 2002, and with the help of Open Access (OA), made the research literature available to the world-wide user community.

Indian ETDs and Repositories

1.	Name	**Mahatma Gandhi University**
	Description	Mahatma Gandhi University Open Access Online Theses Digital Library is an important step towards democratization of knowledge and it is the model of digital archives created by MG University will be emulated by other Indian universities leading to transparency in education research.
	URL	http://www.mgutheses.org/
2.	Name	**Indian Institute of Science**
	Description	This is the digital repository of Theses and Dissertations of Indian Institute of Science, Bengaluru, India. You can search, browse and access theses and dissertations from this collection. This repository has been developed to capture, disseminate and preserve research theses of Indian Institute of Science. It complements ePrints@IISc, the research publications repository of IISc. Number of theses in etd@IISc: 1535.
	URL	http://etd.ncsi.iisc.ernet.in/
3.	Name	**Etheses—A Saurashtra University Library Service**
	Description	Welcome to Etheses, the online archive of Ph.D theses of Saurashtra University. It contains completed and examined Ph.D theses from doctoral candidates who have studied at Saurashtra University. From the 2011-12, session once you have successfully completed your Ph.D.
	URL	http://etheses.saurashtrauniversity.edu/

Cont...

4.	Name	**Dyuthi, Digital Repository of Cochin University of Science and Technology**
	Description	Welcome to Dyuthi, Digital Repository of Cochin University of Science and Technology. Dyuthi is a digital service that collects, preserves, and distributes digital material. Repositories are important tools for preserving an organization's legacy; they facilitate digital preservation and scholarly communication.
	URL	http://dyuthi.cusat.ac.in/xmlui/
5.	Name	**Library of the Indian Institute of Science (JRD Tata Memorial Library)**
	Description	The Library of the Indian Institute of Science (IISc) Bengaluru, was established in 1911. The JRD Tata Memorial Library Annex and Digital Library located opposite NCSI was inaugurated on March 12, 1998 by Mr. Ratan Tata. Some of the library collections like technical reports, standards, patents and theses are located in this building.
6.	URL	http://www.library.iisc.ernet.in
	Name	**North-Eastern Hill University Digital Library**
	Description	The NEHU Central Library at Shillong and the NEHU Campus Library at Tura cater to the needs of the students, research scholars, faculty, administrators and staff of the university. The library building, funded by DoNER, was inaugurated on September 20, 2006 by Shri P.R. Kyndiah, Hon'ble Union Minister of Tribal Affairs & DoNER, Govt.
	URL	http://dspace.nehu.ac.in

Shodhganga: Reservoir of Indian Theses

"Shodhganga" is the name coined to denote digital repository of Indian Electronic Theses and Dissertations set-up by the INFLIBNET Centre. The word "Shodh" originates from Sanskrit and stands for research and discovery. The "Ganga" is the holiest, largest and longest of all the rivers in Indian subcontinent. The Ganga is the symbol of India's age-long culture and civilization, everchanging, ever-flowing, ever-loved and revered by its people, and has held India's heart captive and drawn uncounted millions to her banks since the dawn of history. Shodhganga stands for the reservoir of Indian intellectual output stored in a repository hosted and maintained by the INFLIBNET Centre.

The Shodhganga@INFLIBNET is set-up by using an open source digital repository software called DSpace developed by MIT (Massachusetts Institute of Technology) in partnership with

Hewlett-Packard (HP). The DSpace uses internationally recognized protocols and interoperability standards. Shodhganga provides a platform for research scholars to deposit their Ph.D. theses and make it available to the entire scholarly community in open access. The repository has the ability to capture, index, store, disseminate and preserve ETDs (Electronic Theses and Dissertations) submitted by the researchers.

Shodhganga replicates academic structure of each University in terms of Departments/Centres/Colleges. Each University has to facilitate ease of navigation. This structure facilitates research scholars from universities to deposit their theses in the respective Department/Centre/College. Option for simple search and advance search are available on the home page along with browsing facility through universities and departments. The Centre is also developing a semantic web-based interface to facilitate subject-based browsing, navigation, search and retrieval of contents available in the repository.

Scope and Limitations

Electronic theses in library and Information Science subject submitted by different universities on Shodhganga up to December 5, 2016 is the subject of present study. There were 843 e-theses submitted by 66 universities on Shodhganga.

Data Analysis and Interpretation

Total 843 Ph.D. theses in Library and Information Science subject on Shodhganga repositories were analysed and result of analysis is as follows:

University-wise Contribution of Theses

Researcher found 843 theses uploaded by 67 universities in India on Shodhganga. Among these universities, Karnatak University secured first rank by uploading 90 theses with 10.40% followed by the Aligarh Muslim University securing second rank by uploading 83 theses with 9.60% and third rank secured by Panjab University with contribution of 39 theses in Library & Information Science with 4.51%. Lowest contribution is One theses secured by fifteen universities.

It is concluded that many universities have not uploaded their theses on Shodhganga but few universities like Karnatak University and Aligarh Muslim University are in progressive stage.

Table 1: University-wise Contribution of Theses

Sl. No.	Name Of University	No. of Theses	%	Cumulative No. of Theses	Cumulative %
1	Alagappa University	7	0.81	7	0.83
2	Aligarh Muslim University	83	9.60	90	10.43
3	Andhra University	4	0.46	94	10.89
4	Annamalai University	13	1.50	107	12.39
5	Bangalore University	3	0.35	110	12.74
6	Bharathiar University	37	4.28	147	17.01
7	Bharathidasan University	22	2.54	169	19.56
8	Bundelkhand University	22	2.54	191	22.10
9	Dr. Babasaheb Ambedkar Marathwada University	38	4.39	229	26.49
10	Dr. Harisingh Gour Vishwavidhyalay	2	0.23	231	26.73
11	Gauhati University	20	2.31	251	29.04
12	Gujarat University	1	0.12	252	29.15
13	Gujarat Vidyapith	7	0.81	259	29.96
14	Gulbarga University	8	0.92	267	30.89
15	Guru Ghasidas University	19	2.20	286	33.08
16	Guru Nanak Dev University	6	0.69	292	33.78
17	Indira Gandhi National Open University IGNOU	1	0.12	293	33.89
18	Jadavpur University	1	0.12	294	34.01
19	Jiwaji University	7	0.81	301	34.82
20	Kalasalingam University	1	0.12	302	34.93
21	Kannur University	1	0.12	303	35.05
22	Karnataka State Women's University	2	0.23	305	35.28
23	Karnatak University	90	10.40	395	45.69

Contd...

24	Karunya University	7	0.81	402	46.49
25	Kurukshetra University	11	1.27	413	47.77
26	Kuvempu University	15	1.73	428	49.50
27	Madhya Pradesh Bhoj (Open) University	1	0.12	429	49.62
28	Madurai Kamraj University	1	0.12	430	49.73
29	Maharaja Krishnakumar-sinhji Bhavnagar University	9	1.04	439	50.77
30	Maharaja Sayajirao University of Baroda	7	0.81	446	51.58
31	Mangalayatan University	1	0.12	447	51.70
32	Manglore University	1	0.12	448	51.81
33	Manipur University	23	2.66	471	54.47
34	Manonmaniam Sundaranar University	37	4.28	508	58.75
35	Mizoram University	8	0.92	516	59.67
36	Mother Teresa Women's University	7	0.81	523	60.48
37	North-Eastern Hill University	15	1.73	538	62.22
38	North Maharashtra University	2	0.23	540	62.45
39	Osmania University	4	0.46	544	62.91
40	Panjab University	39	4.51	583	67.42
41	Pt. Ravishankar Shukla University	9	1.04	592	68.46
42	Punjabi University	4	0.46	596	68.92
43	Sambalpur University	7	0.81	603	69.73
44	Sant Gadge Baba Amravati University	13	1.50	616	71.23
45	Sardar Patel University	7	0.81	623	72.04
46	Saurashtra University	1	0.12	624	72.16
47	Savitribai Phule Pune University	7	0.81	631	72.97
48	Shri Jagdishprasad Jhabarmal Tibarewala University	1	0.12	632	73.08

Contd..

49	Singhania University	1	0.12	633	73.20
50	SNDT Women's University	11	1.27	644	74.47
51	Solapur University	1	0.12	645	74.59
52	Sri Krishnadevaraya University	30	3.47	675	78.06
53	Sri Venkateswara University	21	2.43	696	80.48
54	The Gandhigram Rural Institute	3	0.35	699	80.83
55	The IIS University	1	0.12	700	80.95
56	The University of Burdwan	27	3.12	727	84.07
57	Tilak Maharashtra Vidyapeeth	16	1.85	743	85.92
58	University of Calicut	20	2.31	763	88.23
59	University of Delhi	4	0.46	767	88.69
60	University of Jammu	10	1.16	777	89.85
61	University of Kalyani	3	0.35	780	90.19
62	University of Kashmir	4	0.46	784	90.66
63	University of Kerala	23	2.66	807	93.32
64	University of Lucknow	2	0.23	809	93.55
65	University of Mysore	36	4.16	845	97.71
66	Utkal University	19	2.20	864	99.91
67	Veer Narmad South Gujarat University	1	0.12	865	100
Total		**865**	**100.00**		

Year-wise and University-wise Contribution of Theses

Table 2 shows Year-wise and University-wise contribution of theses on Shodhganga repositories. Deposition of theses on Shodhganga started in year 2009 but first two theses in Library & Information Science were deposited by Mizoram University in year 2010. Later on, deposition of theses in year-wise were five in year 2011, 17 in year 2012, 72 in year 2013, 84 in year 2014, 253 in year 2015 and 432 in year 2016. Thus, largest contribution was found in the year 2016 i.e. 432.

Trend of deposition of theses was found at increasing stage i.e. progressive phase which improves open access movement among scholarly communication society.

Table 2: Year-wise and University-wise Contribution of Theses

Sl. No.	Name of University	2010	2011	2012	2013	2014	2015	2016	Total
1	Alagappa University						6	1	7
2	Aligarh Muslim University				4	2	74	3	83
3	Andhra University				3	1			4
4	Annamalai University						9	4	13
5	Bangalore University							3	3
6	Bharathiar University						12	25	37
7	Bharathidasan University			3	1	9	5	4	22
8	Bundelkhand University				18	4			22
9	Dr. Babasaheb Ambedkar Marathwada University							38	38
10	Dr. Harisingh Gour Vishwavidhyalay						2		2
11	Gauhati University					5	2	13	20
12	Gujarat University						1		1
13	Gujarat Vidyapith					4	3		7
14	Gulbarga University					2	3	3	8
15	Guru Ghasidas University				16	1	1	1	19
16	Guru Nanak Dev University					4		2	6
17	Indira Gandhi National Open University—IGNOU							1	1
18	Jadavpur University					1			1
19	Jiwaji University						4	3	7
20	Kalasalingam University							1	1
21	Kannur University							1	1
22	Karnataka State Women's University				1			1	2
23	Karnatak University				3	4	2	81	90
24	Karunya University			1	2			4	7
25	Kurukshetra University				2		8	1	11
26	Kuvempu University					1		14	15

Contd...

27	Madhya Pradesh Bhoj (Open) University		1						1
28	Madurai Kamraj University						1		1
29	Maharaja Krishnakumarsinhji Bhavnagar University				2			7	9
30	Maharaja Sayajirao University of Baroda						6	1	7
31	Mangalayatan University			1					1
32	Manglore University							1	1
33	Manipur University				2	3	18		23
34	Manonmaniam Sundaranar University					9	17	11	37
35	Mizoram University	2						6	8
36	Mother Teresa Women's University					1	3	3	7
37	North-Eastern Hill University						15		15
38	North Maharashtra University						1	1	2
39	Osmania University					3	1		4
40	Panjab University							39	39
41	Pt. Ravishankar Shukla University		1			2	2	4	9
42	Punjabi University		1		2		1		4
43	Sambalpur University						5	2	7
44	Sant Gadge Baba Amravati University				5	3	1	4	13
45	Sardar Patel University						3	4	7
46	Saurashtra University		1						1
47	Savitribai Phule Pune University			6				1	7
48	Shri Jagdishprasad Jhabarmal Tibarewala University							1	1
49	Singhania University							1	1
50	SNDT Women's University			1	4	3		3	11

Contd...

51	Solapur University							1	1
52	Sri Krishnadevaraya University					5	2	23	30
53	Sri Venkateswara University						10	11	21
54	The Gandhigram Rural Institute						1	2	3
55	The IIS University						1		1
56	The University of Burdwan					1	12	14	27
57	Tilak Maharashtra Vidyapeeth			3		3	3	7	16
58	University of Calicut		1		6	4	7	2	20
59	University of Delhi					4			4
60	University of Jammu							10	10
61	University of Kalyani						1	2	3
62	University of Kashmir						4		4
63	University of Kerala			1		1		21	23
64	University of Lucknow					1	1		2
65	University of Mysore			1	1	3	4	27	36
66	Utkal University							19	19
67	Veer Narmad South Gujarat University						1		1
Total		2	5	17	72	84	253	432	865

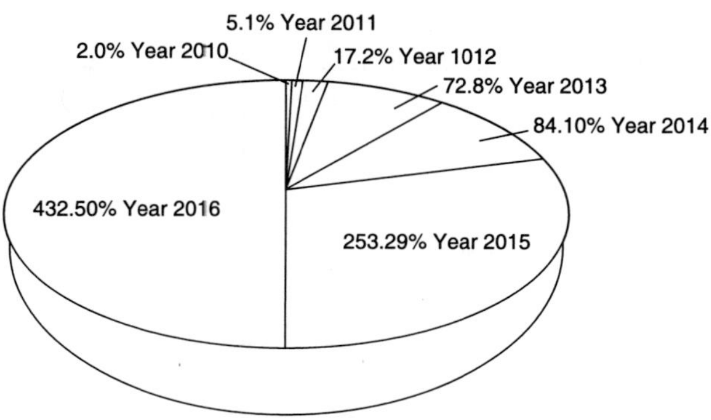

Figure 1: Year-wise Distribution of theses

State-wise Contribution of Theses

No. of universities which have contributed were 67 and these were occupied by 20 States. Tamil Nadu state contributed ten universities as maximum contribution with a percentage of 14.93% followed by Karnataka and Maharashtra with each 7 universities with 10.45%. Lowest no. i.e. one contributed by Assam, Haryana, Manipur, Mizoram and Meghalaya Universities.

Table 3: Year-wise and University-wise Contribution of Theses

Sl. No.	State	No. of Universities	Percentage	Cumulative No.	Cumulative %
1	Tamil Nadu	10	14.93	10	14.93
2	Uttar Pradesh	4	5.97	14	20.90
3	Andhra Pradesh	4	5.97	18	26.87
4	Karnataka	7	10.45	25	37.31
5	Maharashtra	7	10.45	32	47.76
6	Madhya Pradesh	3	4.48	35	52.24
7	Assam	1	1.49	36	53.73
8	Gujarat	7	10.45	43	64.18
9	Chhattishgarh	2	2.99	45	67.16
10	Punjab	3	4.48	48	71.64
11	Delhi	2	2.99	50	74.63
12	Haryana	1	1.49	51	76.12
13	West Bengal	3	4.48	54	80.60
14	Kerala	3	4.48	57	85.07
15	Manipur	1	1.49	58	86.57
16	Mizoram	1	1.49	59	88.06
17	Meghalaya	1	1.49	60	89.55
18	Odisha	2	2.99	62	92.54
19	Rajashthan	3	4.48	65	97.01
20	Jammu & Kashmir	2	2.99	67	100.00
Total		67	100.00		

Findings

It is concluded from analysis that many universities have not uploaded their all the theses on Shodhganga but few universities like Karnatak University and Aligarh Muslim University are in progressive phase. Deposition of theses on Shodhganga started in year 2009 but first two theses in Library and Information Science were deposited by Mizoram University in year 2010. Later on, deposition of theses in year wise were five in year 2011, 17 in year 2012, 72 in year 2013, 84 in year 2014, 253 in year 2015 and 432 in year 2016. Thus, largest contribution was found in year 2016 i.e. 432.

Trend of deposition of theses is found at an increasing stage which improves open access movement among scholarly communication society. Numbers of universities contributed were 67 and these were occupied by 20 States. Tamil Nadu state contributed ten universities as maximum contribution with percentage of 14.93% followed by Karnataka and Maharashtra with each 7 universities with 10.45%. Lowest no. i.e. one contributed by Assam, Haryana, Manipur, Mizoram and Meghalaya Universities.

Conclusion

The present study has attempted to overview the current status of E-theses repositories in India. Out of the various types of institutional repositories, E-theses repositories help in enhancing education and research. Even in the absence of any National Open Access policy in India, on the lines of National Institute of Health (NIH) Policy of the United States, various institutions, academies and scholars are making their research output open access. The ETD repositories should be properly updated and maintained in order to showcase the current research work done. However, key issues such as Intellectual Property Rights and Plagiarism needs to be discussed globally to stop misuse of the scholarly literature available through open access.

References

Budapest Open Access Initiative. 2002. Available: http://www.soros.org/openaccess

Electronic theses and dissertations. Available: http://etd.byu.edu

ETD Guide: Introduction: History of ETD activities. Available: http://curric.dlib.vt.edu/wiki/index.php?title=ETD_Guide:Introduction History of ETD Activities.

Guidelines for the creation of institutional repositories at universities and higher education institutions. Available: www.sisbi.uba.ar/institucional/proyectos/internacionales/Guidelines IR english.pdf

Kothari, C.R. 2004. *Research Methodology*, New Delhi, New Age International Publication.

Shodhganga: A reservoir of Indian theses. 2011. Available:http://shodhganga.inflibnet.ac.in/moredetails/about.html

PART V
LIBRARY SECURITY

17

CCTV Technology for the Security of Libraries

S.N. Chobe

ABSTRACT

CCTV technology is a very important technology in library system. This technology is used in various sections of the library. These sections include reference books section, periodical section, reading room section, book issue counter, computer lab and newspaper section etc. Use of CCTV technology prevents thefts, assaults and other crimes in the library.

Keywords: *CCTV Technology; Monitor; Recorder; Alarm Buzzer.*

Introduction

CCTV technology is such modern technology in which wrong doers are indirectly kept under surveillance and for the further legal actions. It is advanced technique to control and support of good management in the every library. CCTV is a closed circuit television. The first television picture was broadcast in the mid 1930's, by that time, the technology had developed to enable a public television services. It was launched for the first time by the BBC in 1936. Just after a decade, in 1947 an enterprise metropolitan as a police superintendent proposed that the police should be allowed to evaluate the live TV footage of the BBC coverage and the request was refused on the ground of expense but so was born the idea that live television impose could play vital role in routine police system.

In 1950, with the expansion of information and technology these cameras were mainly used for traffic management and in banks and shops. It was only in 1960 that the video technology began to expand in cities mainly in the United Kingdom and United States. In the mid 1990, more affordable system called digital in multiplexing was developed and thus, revolutionized the video surveillance industry. Presently, its starting price is ₹ 15000/75000 in India.

Security measures play vital role in today's insecure world and such technology help us with use of web camera, digital video etc. Such security measures are increasingly used at very important places i.e. cinema hall, shopping mall, hospitals, temples, Parliaments and Assemblies etc. In the same way, CCTV technology is a general security method which is also being used in libraries for internal security of library. Nowadays, libraries are becoming readers centered and providing facilities for the readers. Hence, the readers get free access but notorious people are taking disadvantage of this open access method by theft of invaluable books, journals, periodicals, equipments. Beside, sometimes, employees of the library and got injuries places in library. In all such conditions arrangements of surveillance at entry and exit gate and inside the library are needed.

Requirements for CCTV Technology

1. Computer is essential for CCTV technology.
2. Monitor: Generally it is color, black and white, led etc.
3. Video Camera: Video cameras are changed coupled device in these cameras signals received from lance are covered into imply.
4. Recorder: These should be VCR/TVC 480/500 HVR with high data capacity.
5. Alarm buzzer: CCTV System must have alarms or buzzer so the student/readers who are speaking can be kept under control.
6. Two ways Audio/Video Communication: Two way audio communications is possible in Audio-Video system of CCTV technology.

Use of CCTV Technology in Library Section

1. On library Gate
2. Newspaper Section
3. Periodicals Section
4. Reading Room
5. Textbook Section
6. Reference Book Section
7. Computer Lab

Advantages of CCTV Technology in Library

1. Controlling all Sections in Library.
2. For Smooth Functioning.
3. 24 Hours continuous watch to capture movement and voice.
4. To help the librarian for investigation.
5. Display real time real events accurate place.
6. Prevent theft.

Conclusion

Mostly, in large libraries, expensive textbooks, reference books are available and they implement open access system. At such places, this CCTV technology can solve many problems of security. The library management can also have a watch their routine administration. It is also possible to control the management of library with the help of CCTV cameras.

References

Agarwal, Vibhut. 2000. *Networking Challenges and Opportunities,* Delhi: Rajeet Publication.

Fadke, D.N. 2008. *Granthalaya Sangankikarn ani Adunikikarn,* Kolhapur: Fadke Prakashan.

Kumar, P.S.G. 2003. *Basic Information Technology*; Essa Publication, New Delhi.

Tiwari, Purushottam, *Digital Library,* New Delhi: APH Publication Corporation, pp. 217-24.

18

The Saga of Library Theft and Its Prevention

Harmanpreet Singh Sandhu

ABSTRACT

Each year, libraries lose large amount of valuable books and other materials to thieves. Here's an overview of theft techniques and the ways which can reduce these losses in future by taking preventive steps.

Keywords: *Library Theft; Theft Techniques; Theft Prevention; Biblioklept; Library Security.*

Introduction

You and the circulation desk staff were chatting with patrons or working at terminals as the thief leisurely strolled through the stacks and made his exit through the library's rear door. You should keep it locked, but on hot days like this you prop it open to allow the breeze to cool your workplace. From the record, he has just stolen the latest biography of Karan Johar, three magnificently illustrated works on Indian freedom struggle, and popular hardcover fiction by John Updike, Rushdie, and Amish Tripathi. Not a bad haul, although it's not his biggest or most valuable. He may have removed veritable mountains of items from libraries over the years, and thus, bagged some superb collection of reading material.

Spotting the Crook

In fact, there is not any consistently dependable psychological profile for a book thief. He could be anyone: an elderly woman in a bulky overcoat, a boy with a backpack, or a young mother pushing a stroller. You might assume that street people pose the biggest risk to your collection, but junkies and drunks are not necessarily the most frequent or successful book thieves. Doctors, lawyers, and business leaders have all been caught in the act, as have clergy of every denomination. Students are notorious for library theft, but certain professors are no better. Even school library faculty members have been suspected of stealing: in one case, a professor was investigated for looting his university's special collections division. He was never charged, but his teaching contract was not renewed.

Before you start complaining about the wickedness of the world, consider yourself and your colleagues. Fascinating new titles arrive everyday: have you ever been tempted to take one home and read it before it is processed for general circulation? Isn't such "borrowing" your right as a hard-working professional? Don't you intend to return that title as soon as you've finished it? Isn't reading new titles that arrive a form of professional development?

In most cases, these questions are attempts to justify theft of public property. You are not entitled to take books from your library without going through the standard check-out procedure. Is there a library that allows staff to do so? Has any board approved such a policy?

Why Do They Steal?

There are different motivations for stealing books from libraries, some more pardonable than others. If you've taken home unprocessed titles for a fast read before the public takes its turn and there is no doubt that you will return those titles promptly and in good condition, then your crime hardly merits eternal damnation. If, however, you're selling those titles to second-hand book dealers for extra and untaxed income, you're no better than any other book thief. Theft for resale is common, despite the library's marks of ownership. It's easy to remove many labels and plastic covers, and even if a book is stamped, it is still saleable. Second-hand book dealers are often willing to buy and sell ex-library materials, since to dedicated readers and collectors a former library copy of a desirable title is better than none.

A "withdrawn from collection" stamp reduces the value of a book, but not completely. A first edition of a rare book is attractive, even with labels and stamp impressions. Incidentally, many stamp manufacturers will produce an exact copy of any stamp that your library uses.

Intellectual pack ratting is another motivation for book theft. There is so much to read and understand; there are so many different stories and versions and ways of thinking to investigate. Even if I don't have the time and inclination to study Milton and Dante and William Blake, at least I can have their works on my shelves in preparation for the day when time and inclination coincide and I'm ready to visit their versions of heaven and hell. But books are expensive, and shoplifting from a busy, security-conscious megastore such as Waterstones is risky. So I might as well "borrow" Milton and Co. indefinitely from the library. It's easy to do, and how often do people end up in court for stealing library books? (By the way, has anyone ever served a jail sentence for stealing Milton's *Paradise Lost*?).

Preventive theft occurs most often on university campuses. Jealous Professor abc wants to stop up-and-coming Professor xyz from finishing a research project, publishing a learned article, and securing another large grant. Prof. abc steals certain titles from the university library. He knows that Prof. xyz needs these titles, and now Prof. xyz must obtain them through interlibrary loan, which takes time and adds to his expenses. Using a razor or knife, Prof. abc might also remove articles, diagrams, maps, and tables from other titles that he assumes Prof. xyz will need. As the scramble for research funding becomes more competitive, academic librarians have good reason to fear the increasing depredations of their collections at the hands of Prof. abc or Prof. xyz.

Finally, theft is fun. It's a game, a challenge, a sport. Maneuvering through your collections, avoiding the gaze of the library assistants, careful not to attract the attention of honest patrons, he feels a rush of excitement. This is his way of winning in a world that made him a loser. And it's so much safer than robbing a shop.

How It's Done

A library thief develops a *modus operandi* or style of stealing that includes one or more of the following techniques:

- **Under the coat:** This is a traditional method of concealing items before walking out an exit. "Under the coat" includes hiding items in pockets, tucking them in an armpit, and securing them close to the body under a tightened belt. This is a very effective in libraries without Tattle-Tape systems but not advisable during the hot summer months, since persons in overcoats look suspicious indoors during heat waves.
- **False briefcase compartment:** Usually in the form of a false bottom space or a concealed side pocket. False compartments are good for hiding smaller items, but consider other techniques if you plan to rip off large-format volumes.
- **The chutzpah glide:** As its name implies, this technique requires shameless audacity as well as an ability to keep cool and look inconspicuous. You simply walk out the library exit carrying the items that you're stealing. You make no effort to conceal them. You can tuck scraps of paper in those items to look as though you've marked your place in works that you've been studying for an extended period. You seem to be a mature and serious student.

  Above all, you must appear confident. Your move toward the exit must be calm, unhurried, and nonchalant. You must not attract attention. This technique is effective during busy times when staff is attending to the needs of honest patrons.
- **The unprotected exit:** In libraries, where you are threatened by Tattle-Tape or vigilant staff, unprotected exits are ideal for a fast and inconspicuous departure. Look for side and rear exits, basement doors, and any windows large enough to allow you undetected.
- **The unprotected and unmonitored staff area:** To leave the library by cutting through a staff area

requires chutzpah, but you'd be surprised how easy it is to wander unchallenged through the back rooms, basements, and miscellaneous storage areas of many libraries. There is almost always a staff door through which you and your booty can escape. Some thieves are bold enough to wear a library staff member's identity badge, available from former staff or custom made by the same people who make stamps and other business paraphernalia. Because of high turnover and large on-call staffs in many library systems, it's unlikely that anyone will immediately peg you as a fraud. In fact, well-mannered librarians might offer to direct you to the most convenient exit. After all, good service is the hallmark of the profession.

- **The baby carrier scam:** A variation on the theme of the false briefcase compartment. Traditional prams, strollers and wagons have been employed in successful thefts. The larger the carrier, the more you can carry out, and with a big pram you have room for bulky non-book items such as computer hardware, A-V equipment, and artworks. It's wise to act like a real parent when you use a baby carrier. Take time to adjust that blanket and coo softly at those darling car manuals and CDs that you're about to rip off.
- **Bag and drop:** This technique is frequently used in libraries that employ state-of-the-art Tattle-Tape systems, which are difficult to circumvent. All you need is a bag of some sort to hold the items that you want. When your bag is full, drop it out a window, preferably on a soft and inconspicuous spot such as a bush or a pile of garbage in an open dumpster. If you must drop your bag from a height of several storeys, make sure that it's properly padded to absorb the impact. "Bag and drop" has been used in some of the most impressive library rip-offs. In one notorious case, the thief was spotted dropping his bag by passers-by. Leaving the library, the thief was presented with the bag by a good citizen, who mentioned that it wasn't safe to

drop medieval manuscripts from third-floor windows. The thief agreed and thanked the citizen for his trouble.

- **Scanner avoidance:** Limp in on crutches. Select the books you want and conceal them appropriately. Then ask the circulation desk assistant to let you exit through a side door because you can't negotiate the turnstile, which just happens to employ a Tattle-Tape scanner. The assistant will wish you a speedy recovery as you limp out with your haul. Variations on this theme include the use of wheelchairs, walkers, and electric carts. You can even use a cane, as long as you can communicate to the clerk the idea that passing through that turnstile will cause you pain.
- **Washroom processing:** A washroom cubicle gives you the privacy you need to remove Tattle-Tape or to cut out desirable illustrations, photos, and sections of text. Remember that Tattle-Tape is usually hidden down the spine of a book (a "tweezer job") or pasted onto an inside cover. Tattle-Tape is easily removed from the latter location with a small knife. Once you've removed Tattle-Tape from an item, discard the Tattle-Tape in the used towel bin. Don't leave it lying around the cubicle, since bits of tape will alert library staff to your activities. And it's not smart to flush a large amount of Tattle-Tape down a toilet, since it may clog a pipe, cause a flood, and alert the library staff, etc.

  As for cutting out illustrations with a razor, this is especially common in libraries with collections of old books or high-quality fine arts materials.
- **The visiting dignitary:** Thieves have been using false identities. The visiting dignitary technique has proven successful in numerous libraries as well as museums and art galleries. Usually, the thief purports to be a professor from a prestigious university. He/She appears at the library director's office bearing a phoney business card and forged letters of introduction. May he/she spend a couple of hours in the special collections vault?

Of course he/she's so distinguished and dignified that no one would dream of checking her briefcase for a false compartment. Months later, the library discovers that several valuable manuscripts are missing. The bogus professor has sold them to a crooked book dealer in the United States or Europe for a substantial sum. Since then he/she has hit several other libraries, and no one has questioned his/her letters of introduction or the purpose of his/her research.

In the Event of Capture...

Sometimes the techniques that I've described don't work, and you nab him. What next? In fact, convictions for theft from libraries are rare. Librarians are often disinclined to go through the process of laying charges, going to court, giving evidence, and undergoing cross-examination in a case involving stolen fiction worth under ₹ 1000. Faced with expanding case loads and enormous amounts of paperwork, the police are seldom eager to devote resources to the conviction of a biblioklept. Thus, the risk of a heavy fine or a jail sentence is negligible. Librarians are left to deal with the thieves they catch in the act. They will find the experience frustrating, since there is so little that they can do aside from issuing stern warnings and banning the thief from the library. Catching a thief can be dangerous. To lay hands on someone who is technically innocent of any crime might be considered a violation of rights. Moreover, some thieves are desperate: they might resort to violence, for which few library staff members are prepared. It's easy to understand why so many librarians connive at the activities of thieves.

Preventive Measures

So what can you do to stop biblioklepts? There are eight effective measures to discourage theft in any library. Note that you'll never stop him/her altogether; you'll simply make his/her activities more difficult, and eventually he/she will move on to easier targets. But consider the following preventive measures carefully. Any single measure creates a nuisance for thieves but, when these preventive measures are implemented together, it will be constructive in stopping them altogether.

1. **Tattle-Tape:** There is strong anecdotal evidence across the world that Tattle-Tape reduces library theft. There is probably no better deterrent, especially against amateurs and impulsive thieves.
2. **Signage:** Thieves are discouraged by signs bearing messages such as "advanced security system in operation" and "books are public property". "Thieves will be prosecuted" and "Report all suspicious behavior to the circulation desk". Even a professional thief will be a little nervous about that advanced security system. Is there some new security device in the market that he doesn't know about? Has it been installed in this library? Perhaps it's time to find a branch that isn't so high tech....
3. **Warnings to suspected thieves:** Thieves hate the idea that they're under suspicion. To tell a suspected thief that stealing books is illegal is no violation of one's rights. Other ways of getting across the message:
   - "We keep an eye on people we suspect of stealing, you know."
   - "I'd appreciate it if you didn't carry that bag into the stacks, ma'am."
   - "If you try to pass through the front gates without checking out the books under your coat, sir, an alarm will sound, a very loud alarm."
   - "I wouldn't use that rear door as an exit, chum. I haven't fed my Doberman today, and he's waiting on the landing outside."

   If thieves can employ chutzpah, so can librarians. In fact, a touch of wry humor might be more effective that the sternest warning. You don't need a real Doberman to enhance your security.
4. **Patrols:** An occasional stroll through your library will discourage thieves who depend on a general lack of surveillance, particularly in and around less frequented spaces such as basements, stairwells, and corners of stack areas. Patrolling washrooms is also prudent.

5. **Hardening:** Don't leave doors and windows open that should be locked. Don't allow the public to wander through staff areas. Bolt all computer equipment to supporting surfaces. Make sure that all staff members realize that good security protects them as well as the library's collections. Encourage staff to report all suspicious behavior to library management or on-site security personnel without delay.

6. **Security checks for visiting dignitaries:** He claims to be a professor from IIT. Before you allow him into your special collections vault, check with IIT to see if he's the real thing. One telephone call or e-mail inquiry might save you much grief. Let that professor know that you are obliged to check his identification. If he's a fraud, chances are that he won't stick around for long. If he's impersonating a real professor and he presents top-quality letters of introduction, you can still catch him. One famous thief was caught when a librarian phoned what was assumed to be his residence in Chandigarh. "You say that you're Professor Sangal from RIET, and you want to examine manuscripts," said the librarian. "That's right," said the fraud, with admirable self-possession.

   "I've already given you my card and letters, and I need to see those manuscripts for the purposes of my historical research on the influence of the medieval mathematics." The librarian remained poker faced. "Is that so," she said. "I just spoke to your wife in Chandigarh. She tells me that you died 3 years ago." The fraud left the library in un-professorial haste.

7. **Informing other branches and libraries in neighbouring regions:** If you suspect that a thief is active in your library, let your local colleagues know. If possible, describe them, the thief's appearance and techniques. Some libraries circulate written descriptions of thieves. When a thief realizes that he/she is recognized throughout your system, he/she will move on.

8. **Informing local book dealers:** Share with local book dealers the same information that you give your library colleagues. If dealers refuse to buy suspicious items that might have been stolen from your library, a thief's income will decrease. Dealers are usually happy to cooperate with libraries in frustrating thieves and are grateful when librarians protect them from receiving stolen goods.

Thieves avoid libraries that have a counter beside the front door, angled in such a way that the counter assistant can see most of the shelf area in a single sweeping glance. That assistant can also get a good look at the readers as they enter or exit, which makes thieves uncomfortable. So do library staff who wander around the shelf area and offer assistance. So do stores with securely locked back doors, good lighting, and locked display cabinets for the most expensive stock. Another tactic that annoys crooks is the placement of comfortable chairs in the shelf area. Very clever: you enhance the cozy atmosphere of your store while turning honest customers into unwitting guardians of your stock.

References

Giesecke, Joan. 2010. *Fundamentals of Library Supervision* (2nd ed). Chicago, IL: American Library Association.

Graham, Warren. 2012. *The Black Belt Librarian: Real-World Safety & Security.* Chicago, IL: ALA Editions.

Kahn, Miriam B. 2008. *The Library Security and Safety Guide to Prevention, Planning, and Response.* Chicago, IL: ALA Editions.

Robertson, Guy. 2016. *Robertson on Library Security and Disaster Planning.* Waltham, MI: Chandos Publications.

Shuman, Bruce A. 2002. *Case Studies in Library Security.* Santa Barbara, CA: Libraries Unlimited.

19

Security: Library Intellectual Property

Madan Lal Jat

ABSTRACT

This chapter discusses of the effectiveness of electronic security systems in library and resources with a focus on selected printed and non-printed documents in the all types of Libraries and information canters. This chapter deals with the Electronic Security System i.e. one of the fasted growing and most beneficial technology being adopted by academic, public and special library for increasing efficiency and improving the safety, security, productivity, accuracy and convenience.

Keywords: *Security; Intellectual Property; RFIDs; 3M; EM.*

Introduction

Libraries have changed with the times and so have their collections. Today, the library collection contains a wide variety of materials such as expensive CDs and DVDs, hard-to-replace reference volumes and textbooks, journals, periodicals and magazines.

Without an effective security system in place, many libraries risk the problems associated with the temporary and permanent loss of materials. When items are unavailable, the patrons of your library must do without or go elsewhere. And, although the replacement cost may appear to be low, it is an important factor as it involves the staff time to record, catalogue and process these missing materials, which can double the cost when taken into consideration.

Electronic security systems are devices that are used with the aid of electrical apparatus to secure library materials. They help libraries to control, minimize or avoid library material theft and unethical losses (Rajendran and Rathinasabapathy, 2007). Examples of electronic security systems installed in libraries are electronic surveillance camera (CCTV), 3M electronic security systems (electronic security gates), radio frequency identification (RFID) system, perimeter alarm system, etc.

The objectives of this study are as follows:

I. To know electronic security systems used in the library and information centres.

II. To investigate how library resources are taken out of the library?

III. To find out the different electronic security systems installed in the university libraries under study.

IV. To ascertain the effectiveness of electronic security systems installed in academic libraries under study.

Some Major Security Systems

1. RFID Security Systems
2. 3M Security Systems
3. EM+ RFID Systems
4. EM+ Barcode Systems
5. EM Security Systems

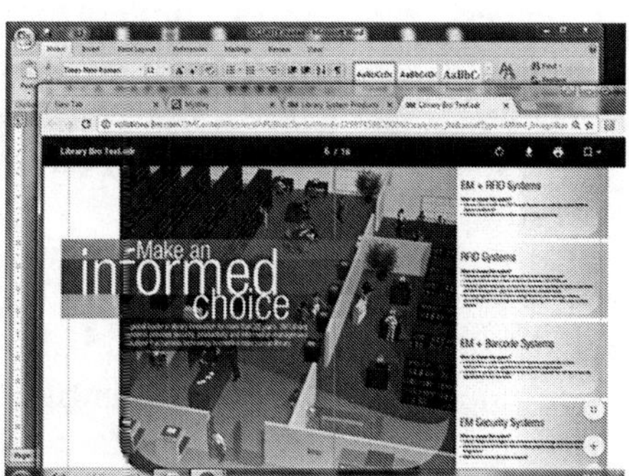

Figure 1: Screen soot of integrated security system

Radio Frequency Identification (RFID)

RFID is a subset of a group of technologies, often referred to as automatic identification, that are used to help machines identify objects, and which include bar codes and smart cards. RFID refers to the subset of automatic identification that uses radio waves to automatically identify bulk or individual items.

In recent years, radio frequency identification technology has moved from obscurity to mainstream applications that helps speed up the handling of manufactured goods and materials. RFID enables identification from a distance, and unlike earlier bar-code technology, it does so without requiring a line of sight. In this chapter, the author introduces the principles of RFID, discusses its primary technologies and applications, and reviews the challenges organizations which will face in deploying this.

What is RFID?

RFID is the reading of physical tags on single products, cases, pallets, or re-usable containers which emit radio signals to be picked up by reader devices. These devices and software must be supported by a sophisticated software architecture that enables the collection and distribution of location-based information in near real time. The complete RFID picture combines the technology of the tags and readers with access to global standardized databases, ensuring real time access to up-to-date information about relevant products at any point in the supply chain.

RFID technologies are grouped under the more generic Automatic Identification (Auto-ID) technologies. Examples of other Auto-ID technologies include Smartcards and Barcodes. RFID is often positioned as next generation bar coding because of its obvious advantages over.

RFID Technology in Libraries

The concept of RFID can be simplified to that of an electronic barcode and can be used to identify, track, sort or detect library holdings at the circulation desk and in the daily stock maintenance. This system, consist of smart RFID labels, hardware and software, provides libraries with more effective way of managing their collections while providing greater customer service to their patrons.

The information contained on microchips in the tags affixed to library materials is read using radio frequency technology regardless of item orientation or alignment. It provides a contact less data link, without need for line of sight.

RFID-based systems have been implemented for efficient document tracking purpose throughout the libraries that combine, easier and faster charging and discharging of documents, security of materials, inventorying, stock verification and shelf handling. RFID tag's transponder listens for a radio query from the reader and responds by transmitting their unique ID code. Most RFID tags have no batteries; they use the power from the initial radio.

Different Types of RFID

Three primary frequency bands are being used for:

- Low Frequency (125/134 KHz)—Most commonly used for access control, animal tracking and asset tracking.
- High Frequency (13.56 MHz)—Used where medium data rate and read ranges up to about 1.5 meters are acceptable. This frequency also has the advantage of not being susceptible to interference from the presence of water or metals.
- Ultra High Frequency (850 to 950 MHz)—offer the longest read ranges of up to 3 meters and high reading speeds.

Figure 2: RF (Radio frequency) detection

RFID System Components and Their Effects in Libraries

Figure 3: Library RFID Management System

An RFID system consists of following:

1. **Tag:** Also known as a transponder, the tag consists of an antenna and silicon chip encapsulated in glass or plastic. The tags contain a very small amount of information. For example, many tags contain only a bar code number and security bit (128 bits) but some tags contain as much as 1024 bits. Tags range in size from the size of a grain of rice to two inch squares depending on their application. Researchers are now working on tags as small as a speck of dust.

   Tags operate over a range of frequencies. Passive tags can be of low frequency (LF) or high frequency (HF). LF tags operate at 125 KHz, are relatively expensive, and have a low read range (less than 0.5 meters). HF tags operate at 13.56 MHz, have a longer read range (approximately 1 meter) and are less expensive that LF tags. Most library applications use HF tags.

   Tags can be Read Only (RO), Write Once Read Many (WORM) or Read Write (RW). RO tags are pre-programmed with a unique number like a serial number (or perhaps eventually an ISBN number). WORM tags are pre-programmed but additional information can be added if space permits. RW tags can be updated dynamically. Sometimes, space on the RW tags is locked where permanent data is kept and the rest of the tag is writable. Most library applications use RW tags.

2. **Readers:** RFID readers or receivers are composed of a radio frequency module, a control unit and an antenna to interrogate electronic tags via radio frequency (RF) communication. The reader powers an antenna to generate an RF field. When a tag passes through the field, the information stored on the chip in the tag is interpreted by the reader and sent to the server, which, in turn, communicates with the integrated library system when the RFID system is interfaced with it.

   RFID exit gate sensors (readers) at exits are basically two types. One type reads the information on the tag(s) going by and communicates that information to a server. The server, after checking the circulation database, turns on an alarm if the material is not properly checked out. Another type relies on a "theft" byte in the tag that is turned on or off to show that the item has been charged or not, making it unnecessary to communicate with the circulation database.

   Readers in library RFID systems are used in the following eight ways:

   - Conversion station—Where library data is written to the tags.
   - Staff workstation at circulation—Used to check-in and check-out materials.
   - Patron self-check-out station—Used to check-out books without staff assistance.
   - Exit sensors—Verify that all books leaving the library have been checked out.
   - Patron self-check-in station—Used to check-in books without staff assistance.
   - Book drop reader—Checks in books when patrons drop them in the book drop.
   - Sorter—Automated system for returning books to proper area of library.
   - Portable reader—and held reader for inventorying and verifying that items are shelved properly.

3. **Antenna:** The antenna produces radio signals to activate the tag and read and write data to it. Antennas are the channels between the tag and the reader, which controls the system's data acquisitions and communication. The electromagnetic field produced by an antenna can be constantly present when multiple tags are expected continually. Antennas can be built into a door frame to receive tag data from person's things passing through the door.
4. **Server:** The server is the heart of some comprehensive RFID systems. It is the communications gateway among the various components. It receives the information from one or more of the readers and exchanges information with the circulation database. Its software includes the SIP/SIP2 (Session Initiation Protocol), APIs (Applications Programming Interface), NCIP or SLNP necessary to interface it with the integrated library software. The server typically includes a transaction database so that reports can be produced.

Role of Librarians

RFID technology introduces an ethical dilemma for librarians. The technology allows greatly improved services for patrons especially in the area of self-check-out, it allows for more efficient use of professional staff, and may reduce repetitive stress injuries for library workers. And yet, the technology introduces the threat of hot listing and tracking library patrons. Librarians have taken extra steps to ensure that laws such as the USA PATRIOT Act cannot be used by government entities to invade the privacy of their patrons, and yet many of those same libraries are placing traceable chips on their patron's books.

Libraries have traditionally acted to protect and defend the privacy of their patrons and yet some are implementing a technology before proper safeguards have been developed. Library use of RFID technology serves to legitimize the technology in the eyes of the community. Therefore, it is incumbent on the library community to ensure that the technology is developed in concert with established privacy principles and that any library use of RFID follows best practices guidelines consistent with library values.

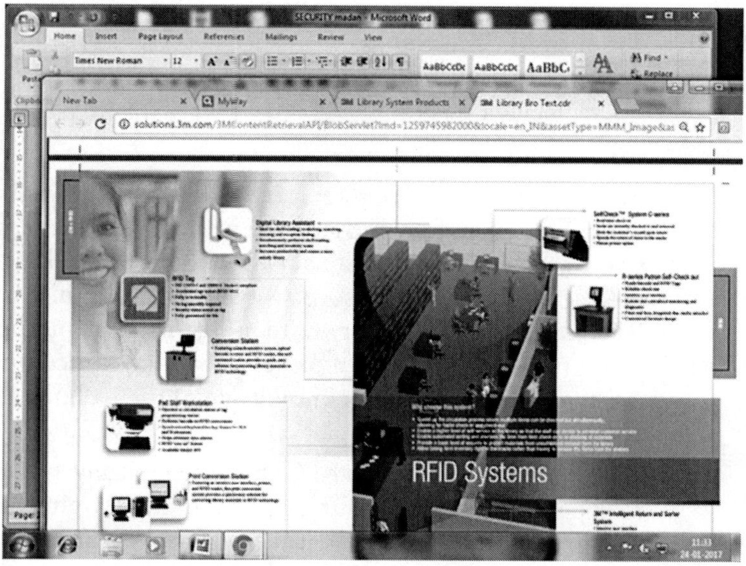

Screen soot of RFID system

Figure 4: RFID systems

Advantages of RFID for Libraries

RFID tags replace both the bar code and traditional security systems and creating a “smart library”.

- Check-out stations can be automated with easy, intuitive interfaces, since several items in a pile cane “grabbed” at a time.
- Book returns can be automated with check-in and database updates completed simultaneously in the book return chute.
- Fast and convenient on-the-shelf inventory allows accuracy in collection management.
- Automatic book sorting.
- Reduce material handling time.
- Does more frequent and accurate inventory to better manage the collections.

- Improve ergonomics of the repetitive tasks of librarians.
- Improve customer service and others services.

Disadvantages of RFID Systems

- **High cost:** The major disadvantage of RFID technology is its cost. While the readers and Gate sensors used to read the information typically cost.
- **Accessibility to compromise:** It is possible to compromise an RFID system by wrapping the protected material in two to three layers of ordinary household foil to block the radio signal. It is also possible to compromise an RFID system by placing two items against one another so that one tag overlays another. That may cancel out the signals. This requires knowledge of the technology and careful alignment.
- **Removal of exposed tags:** RFID tags are typically affixed to the inside back cover and are exposed for removal. This means that there would be problems when users become more familiar with the role of the tags. In Indian libraries, it is a major challenge to keep the tags intact.
- **Exit gate sensor (Reader) problems:** While the short-range readers used for circulation charge and discharge and inventorying appear to read the tags the performance of the exit gate sensors is more problematic. They always don't read tags placed at up to twice the distance of the other readers.

3M Library System

Library Systems from 3M enables customers to learn, explore, discover and grow. Its productivity, security and information management solutions provides innovative and effective tools to ensure that library personnel spend less time on routine tasks and more time with customers.

The system provides a mixed blend of security and information management solutions and leadership in library systems which promotes efficiency and ensures consumer satisfaction.

3M detection systems ensures that no any material leave the library without being checked out. They are safe for magnetic media, comply with the ADA, have audible/visible alarms.

Fact of 3M Library Security System

Commitment: 3M was founded in 1902 and it has been providing library solutions for over 38 years.

Service: It is committed to satisfy libraries with superior quality, value and service respect.

Global Reach, Local presence: With their global reach and local presence, libraries assured that its responsive teams will be there to assist, wherever and whenever.

Pride: It is consistently rated as one of the most respected companies due to its ethics and community service.

Community: It support the library community in a variety of ways including sponsoring the annual NMRT scholarships and millions in donations globally as a company.

Innovation: They are committed to innovation and research.

3M Quality Commitment

The system provides commitment to quality in two ways: The 3M™ Tattle-Tape™ Security Strip and 3M™ RFID Tag Warranty. It stand behind the quality of our library systems, products and make sure you are satisfied. They have been the global leader in library security, productivity and information management systems for over 38 years. 3M Systems help the libraries all over the world to keep their materials safe and available to customers.

Figure 5: 3M security systems

In the Performance Warranty anyone have nothing to lose. When anyone buy 3M Library Systems products with a one year Service Agreement, they have one full year of warranty on the products. Because 3M is the right choice. Consumables and non-3M branded products are excluded from this Performance Warranty.

Conclusion

Security base technology promises to change our world. It has the capability of making our personal lives and our work lives in the library more convenient. However, every new technology comes at a cost. In order to remediate those costs, efforts must be undertaken to guide its development and implementation. Libraries should not yet implement security systems.

Libraries that choose to implement Security system as RFID technologies in advance of policy safeguards being put in place should take extra precautions to follow evolving best practices guidelines. Libraries should continue to protect privacy by ensuring that they are not seen as proponents of RFID before it can be safely deployed. Libraries should work to ensure that RFID products are manufactured and used according to well-established privacy principles. They should refuse to implement potentially unsafe RFID solutions simply. Finally, libraries must be outspoken in their public education efforts related to electronic security systems as RFID, EM+ RFID, EM+ Barcode systems, and 3M.

References

Chavan, Subhash P. 2012. *Use of RFID Technology in Libraries. Online International Interdisciplinary Research Journal*, {Bi-Monthly}, Volume-II, Issue-IV.

http://www.eff.org/Privacy/Surveillance/RFID/20031002_sfpl_comments.php accessed on 21-23 Jun., 2017.

Osayande, Odaro. Electronic Security Systems in Academic Libraries: A Case Study of Three University Libraries in South-West Nigeria. *Chinese Librarianship: An International Electronic Journal,* 32.

Sarma, E.S., Weis, S.A. and Engels, D.W. 2002. *RFID systems, security and privacy implications.* Cambridge, MA: Massachusetts Institute of Technology, AUTO-ID Center.

Syed, Shahid. 2005. Use of RFID Technology in Libraries: a New Approach to Circulation, Tracking, Inventorying, and Security of Library Materials. Library Philosophy and Practice. 8(1).

Tien, Lee. 2003. Privacy risks of radio frequency identification "tagging" of library books. Electronic Frontier Foundation.

20

Security Systems in Libraries

R. Pommal Rao

ABSTRACT

The assets of a Library include all types of tangible property such as books, periodicals, archives, computers, microforms, special collections, art work, and other valuables. Intangible assets also such as computer programs, internal and external databases consisting valuable information. In addition, some libraries may have rare books, institutional repository, unpublished manuscripts of the faculty and laboratory manuals, etc. These assets which have under weak protection because of open access facility being followed in big libraries or assets which are out of proper care attracts to steal. Librarians are experiencing loss of any above asset especially reading materials during periodical stock verifications. The concerned costs towards loss of books are huge in some libraries. The librarian is a custodian of public property in all types of libraries.

This chapter describes the possibility of theft of collection from the libraries, situations for theft and similar issues. It unveils the necessity of installing electronic security systems which have drastically improved the situation. The problems in general which were identified by the librarians either in manual system or in an electronic security system are also incorporated. Chapter also examines the effectiveness of electronic gadgets. Further the safety of library staff and building also discussed.

Keywords: *Libraries—Security Issues; Libraries—Theft of Books—Prevention; Protection—Library Assets.*

Introduction

Library is a public property. Not only the libraries which are functioning under the State or Central Governments, the libraries which are functioning under private associations or corporate bodies also treated as public properties, because the information storage is for all and public utility. Preservation of knowledge is needed for both present and future generations. Security is required for all kinds of libraries and the librarian or library manager, library staff, library users, visitors, and the library committee are equally responsible to protect library properties.

There are few minor differences between terminology. Security and safety may be studied in combination. Security is the degree of resistance to, or protection from harm. It applies to any vulnerable and valuable asset. For example in general, worthy ornaments well exposed in public may have risk and receives threat. Asset means something valuable that an entity (individual, corporation or country) owns. Assets can be divided into two groups, (1) tangible assets, and (2) intangible assets. There are many examples for tangible (physical touchable materials) assets, such as buildings, lands, cash, books, bonds, debentures, savings accounts, etc. Computer programs, databases, etc. are called as intangible assets. The assets, such as items, data, human efforts, etc. which has under weak protection or out of proper care attracts to steal.

Safety can be defined as the control of recognized hazards to achieve an acceptable level of risk. A Natural Hazard is a natural phenomenon that might have a negative effect on people or on the environment. Natural Hazard refers to all atmospheric, hydrologic, geologic (seismic and volcanic), and wildfire phenomena which affects humans, their structures, or their activities harmfully. Safety can be handled either through manual or with the machines.

Why Security Required for Libraries

Loss of reading materials is a common phenomenon in all kinds of libraries. Various reasons exist for loss of reading materials in libraries. Few situations are listed below:

Open Access System: Readers do not have freedom to go into the stack area, where closed access is followed. Readers have liberty to refer books and select the required reading material on their own, where open access is available. Open Access creates problem.

Transactions: Lending of books is an important prevalent function in all types of libraries. A book is issued out and taken back multiple times through the circulation section. Either in manual operated or computer operated circulation system, hundreds of transactions may occur in a day such as issues, reissues (renewals) and returns. Automated circulation system is also required to be run by the manpower. There is a chance to mis-handle or mis-feed the entries while issuing and returning of books. Mis-handling at the time of issuing creates a problem. Book, once issued out which are not recorded properly can be treated as lost, hence they may be returned or may not be returned by the user whether the user is familiar with checking own account. These situations could be controlled by adopting security systems in which activation and deactivation scanner is a part.

Theft of Reading Materials: Among all types of reading materials, books are more likely to be from the libraries. Library users in extraordinary situations, commit book theft. When their access level for borrowing of books is over and still they require a book urgently, there is a chance to book theft. In many big libraries circulation section closes after office hours 5.00 P.M. or 5.30 P.M. and library closing time will be beyond that. When a book is required and the user is unaware about the closing of circulation section, he/she tries to take out the book from the library. In academic libraries, it may be normal practice during examinations. In addition to all these situations, hobby of book theft may disturb the conservation of reading materials.

Anyway a book which is taken out for any reason without entry at the circulation desk can be treated as lost. If a patron sincerely bringing the book back to the library in a situation 'the work has been completed by him', the incidence will be accountable. As per the UGC guidelines regarding book theft, the pattern says that 4 books are allowed against every 1000 transactions at the circulation desk. However, if these books are also protected from theft, the Library and Information Centres may be praised towards right and perfect conservation of reading material for future generations.

Tool for estimating the loss of books is Stock Verification. Libraries conducts stock verification every year to verify the acquired reading materials (whether purchased or gifted) are totally available in the library or not in a particular period. Small libraries undertake stock verification every year. Big libraries especially, University libraries and State Central libraries conducts partial stock verification phase wise, but completes within 5 years. The stock verification reports are required to submit to the higher authorities and audit parties in all libraries. According to these reports, the librarians plan for adopting future controlling mechanism for book theft. Few such measures are: (1) welding of wire mesh to the windows, (2) using one door for entry and exit and closing other doors, if any, (3) increasing access levels during examinations, (4) providing quality photocopy facilities within the library, (5) extending of circulation section timings, and at least keeping the issue counter open.

Library Assets and Security Measures

According to the said tangible and intangible assets, the Library Security can be divided into two, (1) Physical Security, (2) Data Security.

Physical Security

Library physical security can be handled through manual security measures and with the support of a security machines (systems).

Manual Security

All kinds of libraries were depending on manual security in the recent past and the security related functionalities were being attended by persons only. The persons posted at security counter(s) of the library were looking after the functions like (1) Verification of identities of library users at the entrance while entering into the library, (2) Restriction of personal belongings at the entrance, (3) Checking the belongings while going out of the library, (4) Going around surrounding areas of the library to find out thrown books if any, (5) Attending training on operating 'Fire Extinguishers' and handling in extraordinary situations, etc.

Librarians or Library Managers were facing many challenges while controlling different student personalities while utilizing library services. Librarians worried too much in some extraordinary situations at the time of handling security verifications. Sometimes, some students and faculty may feel bad towards checking all the belongings including their pockets, etc. There are evidences of fighting situations with the security and library staff in several university libraries.

Problems in Manual Security

The followings are some of the major problems faced by all kinds of libraries in which manual security exists:

(a) **Shift duties:** Many libraries especially, university libraries are functioning more than 12 hours a day. Even the staff members are attending various shift duties (morning, regular, evening and night), employees feel more convenience in regular shift duty i.e., during office hours. Because of non-availability of transport, food consumption in odd hours and for other problems employees feel inconvenient and uncomforted while delivering other shift duties. Sometimes, real problem may not be existed, people psychologically diverts themselves into frustration.

(b) **Relievers:** This problem exists while performing shift duties. For example; where first shift starts at 8.00 A.M. and closes by 3.00 P.M.; 2nd shift starts at 3.00 P.M. and closes by 10.00 P.M.; the staff posted in 2nd shift have to relieve the 1st shift attended staff at 3.00 P.M. Due to negligence and other causes, problem persists when 2nd shift employees won't come on time to relieve the 1st shift staff. And simply the 1st shift staff can't leave the entrance/exit gate without handing over to 2nd shift employee. This situation prompts an employee into irritation and diversion of attention.

(c) **Sleeping:** For laziness or some other situations when the night shift staff posted in morning shift on immediate next day diverts the attention of security employees. Some other times the absent-minded employees (eyes may be opened but mind somewhere else can be commonly observed). This situation may occur due to personal problems and family disturbances, etc. All these situations sidetrack the employees working at library security gate towards sleeping or semi-sleeping.

(d) **Feeling tired:** There is no uniformity in human health conditions. Health condition changes every day. Not only the library employees, many employees utilizes their casual, restricted, earned or medical leave for major or minor requirements. After having no balance leaves in credit to utilize when the employee feels bodily uncomfortable, this situation arises. This is also a reason to weak verification of library users, at the time of entry and exit.

(e) **Complete Absence (Leave Periods):** Employees are supposed to inform their concerned library authorities regarding utilization of various leaves well in advance. This information is essential to make substitute arrangements by the library executives who deal with library administration. Few library employees neglect the office procedures and practices and suddenly utilize leaves by making phone calls. Even some won't inform on same day and joins next day by submitting an application after utilization of leave. This situation gives trouble to library administration.

(f) **Favouritism (Friends, Relatives, Known Persons and others):** Not total employees influenced by favouritism, but few employees in extraordinary situations shows this while attending to library requirements of friends, relatives, known persons, whereas strict towards unknown library users. This attitude prompts to lose library properties and reflects failure of manual security.

Electronic Security

Keeping in view of super malls, jewellery shops, museums and crowd places, security systems have been invented to overcome these problems which are faced in manual security. Later these systems were manufactured by many companies throughout the world and being adapted at several other places. Many studies determined about good quality performance of the security systems.

The librarians also impressed with the successful functioning of security systems and found suitable for restricting the access of unauthorised persons into the libraries. In later stages, several other security related systems have entered the libraries as well as into our daily. Not only in libraries, these systems were being installed at public places and are being used by Traffic Police, Banks, Railway Platforms, and Air Ports, etc.

Related Issues

- **Required for big libraries:** Patrons (Library Users) will be more in university libraries and apex public libraries in a State. According to their strength, daily visitors and daily circulation transactions are more. In addition to manual security, security systems are more useful.
- **Library has to meet high expenditure:** Manufacturing costs are more and more. In addition to buying the system, entire library collection has to be well prepared for activation and de-activation. EM (Electro Magnetic) tags are required to be inserted in books. Each such tag costing around ₹ 4-6 each. EM Tags will be silent or nonfunctional, in case of buying a new security system after several years, and required to replace with new.
- **Power required uninterrupted:** As mentioned said, Security Systems won't function during power failures. Hence, libraries have to purchase UPS (Uninterrupted Power Systems) and should enter in to AMCs (Annual Maintenance Contracts) for successful functioning. Solar System installation may be an alternative instead of buying more UPS units.

- **Functions without bias once fixed/installed:** This is an advantage to libraries. A VIP can influence security personnel on duty. Security Systems function irrespective of genders and designations.
- **Accurate Results:** Can be expected for initial years of installation.
- **Users lost their privacy:** This may be a problem from users' side. This problem persists with CCTV only.

Problems in Electronic Security

The followings are some of the major problems faced by all kinds of libraries in which only electronic security exists:

(a) **Power Failures:** It is well known problem to all the librarians. Systems won't function during power failures. Whether uninterrupted power systems are required or a solar power unit is needed to install to overcome this problem during power failures.

(b) **Stoppage of un-authorised carrying out of Books:** System produces beep sound when a library user tries to take out an activated book (EM Tag inserted) without presenting it to the Circulation Counter. Its duty completes while detecting an activated/deactivated book and observing silence for deactivated books and producing beep sound for activated books. It won't held-up any malpracticing user.

(c) **Alarms when unnecessary:** Security systems produces beep sounds while carrying out electronic materials, digital watches, etc. More than the required beep sounds create sound pollution in the library.

(d) **Malfunctioning:** In general, performance reduces day by day for any machine or electronic system. Everybody's experience that the glairiness of color TV exhausts after 4-5 years. Touch screen of mobile also do not respond after maximum usage. Similarly, the performance of security systems changes after certain period.

Hence, the libraries are required to replace the old security system with new system after undertaking evaluation process (5-7 years approximately) and to bear suitable big budget.

Which is Suitable to Libraries?

Librarians have to decide themselves about the suitability of security systems for their libraries. Many libraries functioning in corporate institutions, such as engineering colleges, medical colleges, pharmacy colleges, etc. are simply moving towards installing security systems in their libraries and do not care about the requirement, suitability, cost effectiveness and compatibility, etc. This may happen due to competitiveness among corporate institutions while fixing the collecting fees.

Manual security and Electronic security measures are equally required for university libraries to control book theft.

Security Gadgets

Gadgets/Systems for managing physical security which is essential for protecting Library properties especially the Library collection can be subdivided according to the functioning technologies:

Access Control/Authentication—is the selective restriction of access to a place or other resource. The act of accessing may mean consuming, entering, or using. Permission to access a resource is called Authorization. Prevention is better than cure. Once simply allowing the library users, later, facing problem to send them out at the time of detecting misappropriation is a burden. Authenticity of library users can be controlled at the time of entry into libraries at initial level itself. Right of entry can be controlled through various gadgets, like Metal Detectors, Turn Style systems, Swift Track Pedestrian Barriers, Biometric systems (Finger/Face/Pupil Readers), Electronic Surveillance Systems, RFID, Cards and Readers, and Passwords, etc.

Turn Style Systems—is used for access control solutions. These systems utilize Radio Frequency Identification technology to identify people and objects. This enables libraries to monitor the passage of every individual entering and leaving through a facility.

Main Power

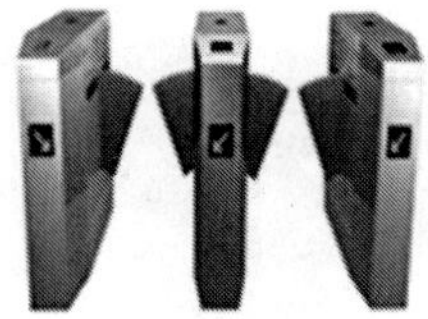

Systems

Systems

Finger Print Readers

Biometric Lock

Biometric Lock

Iris Readers

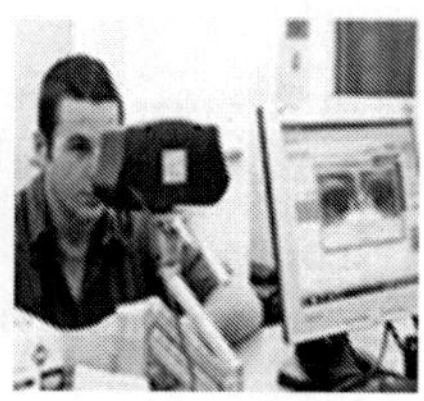

Face Closed

Reader Circuit

Various Models of Turn Style Systems

Biometric Systems—Persons/users can be identified with measurable biological characters like finger print reading, face identification, pupil reading, etc. Ultimate Time and Attendance Solutions recognizes people using physical characteristics of hand geometry to identify an individual. Closed Circuit Television—is latest digital surveillance technology and can incorporate features such as thermal imaging, motion detection, and providing remarkable performance in libraries to closely observe the movements of library patrons while utilizing library services.

RFID Technology—is used for auto theft detection, self-check-out & check-in operations at the circulation and high speed inventory in libraries. RFID Tags replaces both the electro-magnetic tags and bar codes.

RFID Self Check Work Station **Hand held Scanner**

Figure 2: CCTV (Closed Circuit Tele Vision) Camera Models

STPB (Swift Track Pedestrian Barriers)—Controls constant flow of Pedestrians passing through the bars.

- **Alerting Systems:** Burglary Alarming Systems such as Door Opening Alarms, Windows Opening Alarms and Glass Break Detectors whose functions are based on sensor devices fitted inside.
- **Safety Systems:** Fire Extinguishers, Smoke Detectors and Fly Catchers, etc. are useful in extraordinary and unwanted situations.

HVAC (Heating, Ventilation, and Air Conditioning) and other conservative technologies such as Fumigation, De-acidification (Degrading of paper by Neutralizing Acids), Micro-Filming, Laminating, DEZ (Di Ethyl Zinc) Process, Foxing, Binding, etc. are also required for Collection Security, but differs from the above study.

References

Jadhav, Mahendra N. and Shobha Kulkarni. Electronic security; a case study of IIT Bombay central library. Retrieved from http://ir.inflibnet.ac.in/bitstream/1944/181/2/03cali_12.pdf on 27.1.2017.

Lorenzen, Michael G. 1996. Security issues of academic libraries. Retrieved 27 Jan. 2017 from: http://files.eric.ed.gov/fulltext/ED396765.pdf.

Mandal, Achintya K. and Nandi, Subodh Gopal. Biometric recognition; novel approach for library patron authentication. Proceedings of ICAL '09. pp. 694-97.

Osayande, Odaro. Electronic Security Systems in Academic Libraries; a case study of three University Libraries in South-West Nigeria. Chinese Librarianship, an international electronic journal, V.32, 2011.

Rathinasabhapathy, G. (et al.). Biometric Applications in Library and Information Centres: Prospects and Problems. Proceedings of 6th International CALIBER 2008, held at University of Allahabad. pp. 182-89.

Tharun Mothukuri and Gouthami Velakanti. 2011. Biometrics security system for libraries. In Library security management in digital era, proceedings of the national conference NCLSM 2011, (pp. 305-16). Hyderabad: JNTUH.

Uma, V., Susheela, V.J. and Babu, V. Nireekshana. 2010. Electronic Security Systems in University Libraries with special reference to IGM Library, University of Hyderabad. *Pearl: A Journal of Library and Information Science.* 4(1), 13-20.

Part VI
MISCELLANEOUS

21

Modern Libraries and Learning Resource Centres Empowering Scholars

Narender Kumar

ABSTRACT

Since the dawn of the human civilization, libraries have been playing a vital and a significant role in the development of the society, in particular and nation, in general. It has been observed in many studies that scholars consecutively, requires current information related to their core areas so that they may proceed further in their research and they even require material published in journals of national and international repute. It is well known fact that the knowledge which prevails inside the libraries is authentic one. The scholars may access the databases according to their required schedule. As per famous proverb 'knowledge is wealth'. Scholars always keep themselves busy to do something new in their core areas and library remains helpful for them. It won't be an exaggeration to say that an empowering mind can contribute in the development of academics, societies, villages, states, and nation. In the present time, libraries and information centres really got changed in their orientation due to emerging technologies. The present chapter will try to explain the role of modern libraries in empowering the scholars.

Keywords: *Library; Empowering minds; Scholars; Academics; Technologies.*

Introduction

From ancient time, libraries are the hub of contents and having substantial value among academicians as they always keep abreast with latest developments and help in their academic research activities. However, the system of information retrieval was manual and time consuming with traditional libraries. But in the modern time, due to emergence of information and communication technology in the library systems, the information has reached at the threshold of end users. The researchers can access and download the information with minimum possible time whether it is published in any corner of the world. The distance does not matter in the age of ICTs. The electronic resources are available in crore, and accessible on subsidized prices. Library consortiums are available. Moreover, if any institution, college and university faces the problem of budget, the resource sharing facility is also available for them. In the present time, libraries and centres are available in the form of hybrid, digital, electronic, and virtual. Even through mobile apps, the scholars may access the concerned library. These services are really mind blowing and empowering.

Modern Libraries are the Hive of Digital Contents

Before incorporating the digital contents, we must have to realize the need for digital contents and advantage of digitization for libraries. Then it would be easy to understand the role of digital contents to empower the libraries and scholars.

What's the Need of the Digitization?

Digitization has strong presence in the present academic societies. The present scholars cannot survive without digital contents as delivery of the same is very fast even accessible round the clock throughout the year. Nevertheless, it has been identified that there are three prime needs of digitization:

- **To preserve the documents lifetime and for perpetual access:** In the print form, every document has its life span, after completing the lifespan, the concerned documents lead to heelpiece position. However, digitization is the solution to preserve the documents for lifetime. It gives the freedom to scholars to access the relevant material without any restriction.

- **To make the documents more accessible:** Digitization gives more access to documents due to online availability. It requires only the IT infrastructure.
- **To reuse the documents:** Digitized documents can be reused as documents by converting them into different formats.

Digitization of documents is a long-term process which includes physical efforts, finance and time. Once get it, numerous benefits may be counted and seen.

Advantages of Digitization for Libraries

Digitization is having countless benefits. Even, it is the value addition in library services. Some fundamental benefits are as under:

- Quick and efficient circulation operations
- Enhanced security for library items
- Seamless inventory management
- Emerging technology experience for library staff and patrons.

Although latest nascent technologies have put forth so many new challenges in front of the modern libraries but due to welcome by libraries and library professionals, as of now, the libraries have become the hive of digital contents. The scholars are enjoying the speed of contents delivery. With jet speed, things are being changed. The countless digital contents are available. Some important are here:

- **Digital contents developed under the aegis of information and library network (INFLIBNET):** The main objective of the e-ShodhSindhu Consortia for Higher Education E-Resources is to provide access to qualitative electronic resources including full-text, bibliographic and factual databases to academic institutions at a lower rates of subscription. An e-ShodhSindhu is a joint venture of Infonet and INDEST. With this venture, the databases are available on subsidized prices and huge amount of information is available on single platform. There is no need to make any negotiation with publishers as prices of the available databases is fixed after negotiating under e-ShodhSindhu project. The following programmes have been started by the INFLIBNET which are really the hub of digital contents and thereby day by day, the academic societies are marching towards digitization.

- **Shodhganga:** A reservoir of Indian theses: It is a wonderful initiative of INFLIBNET. On this platform, the soft copies of Indian theses are available only of those universities who have signed on MoU with the INFLIBNET for Shodhganga Repository. It is very helpful for research scholars as scholars may avoid the duplicate work. The system is user friendly and very easy to access the theses of different universities. So far 157157 theses and 3900 synopses have been uploaded into Shodhganga repository and 328 universities have signed MoU and 295 universities have contributed. These uploaded theses shall help to rising scholars in order to decide the titles and scope of their forthcoming research. One major benefit is to avoid the duplicacy in research as huge database at single platform may help to avoid the duplicate title. Hence, this is commendable service of Shodhganga repository.
- **N-List:** This program is also the hub of digital contents. Its prime objective is to enhance the usability of e-resources amongst the academic colleges. For its membership, very nominal fee is required to be paid by the concerned college. It gives access to millions of books, journals and magazines. The database is very useful for college students. The home page of the same is also very attractive and user friendly:

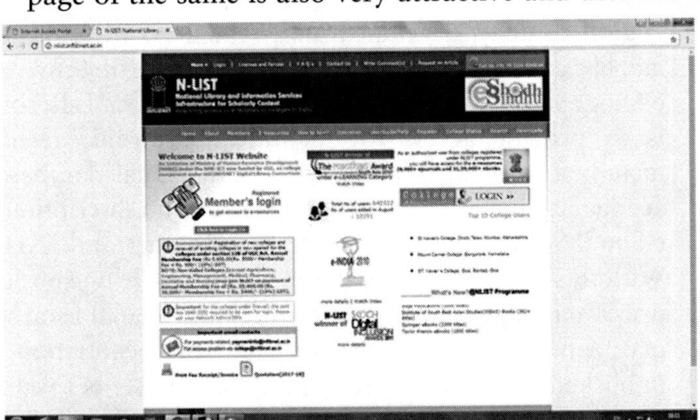

- **Vidyanidhi:** This program was started in 2000 by the Department of Library and Information Science, University of Mysore, with the sponsorship of National Information

System for Science and Technology. It contains the electronic theses and dissertations.

- **Krishi Prabha:** It is database for electronic theses and dissertations of Indian Agricultural Universities. It is the first of its kind in agricultural research.

Some Other Digital Contents which Really Strengthen and Empower the Scholars

Since ancient time, the prime objective of the libraries is to empower the scholars by offering the latest services in their core area. As of now, the technologies are emerging per day by day which have changed the orientation of the libraries as modern scholars do not need to visit frequently; they get the information at their mobile phones or desktop. To cope up with this approach, the digital contents are the inevitable need of the modern libraries and learning resource centres.

- **National Program on Technology Enhanced Learning:** NPTEL is playing a very fundamental role. It is a joint program of IITs and IIScis. Presently, IIT Bombay is looking after this program. Under this program, more than 18000 video lectures are freely available on web. The author personally took the feedback from the users about the quality of the videos. The feedback received by the author is really remarkable. The lectures cover mostly all disciplines like, engineering and technology, humanities, sciences, and management. The scholars can easily download the same and may listen off-line also.
- **Gyan-Darshan:** The initiative was taken in 2000 for school kids, university students, and adults.
- **Gyan-vani:** It was started in 2000 by IITs and IGNOU.
- **E-Gyankosh:** It is launched in 2005 by IGNOU. The objective of the program is to provide open access to self-learning materials.
- Creation of e-content for 996 courses in Phase-II in Engineering, Sciences, Technology, Humanities, and Management by IIT Madras.
- UGC has already cleared a proposal to publish e-content for 77 postgraduate courses.

- IIT-Bombay has started the program of Centre for Distance Engineering Education Program (CDEEP) where the virtual classroom is created and interaction is done through real time interactive satellite technology.
- **MOOC in India:** India is a developing country and trying to practise MOOC. The Hon'ble Prime Minister of India has launched a program i.e. SWAYAM—Study Webs of Active Learning for Young Aspiring Minds. For the same, a MoU has been signed with US Department of State vide which the US universities have offered online courses through this platform. In addition, Sakshat is a part of national mission which is operated by Government of India. As of now, only top academic institutes like IITs and IIMs have been offering online courses under MOOC.
- **National Digital Library:** It is the biggest level initiative and IIT Kharagpur is responsible to complete this task. Through this program study material is being offered from primary level to higher education level. Anyone can become the member of this program. There are two ways to take the membership. One is individual membership and other is institutional membership. Millions of books, magazines, biographies, autobiographies, journals and videos are available on single platform. Thereon, fully downloadable.

Conclusion

Modern libraries must be equipped with digital contents and state-of-the-art facilities so that better and timely services may be offered to scholars and achieve its prime objective which is to satisfy the end users. Undoubtedly, modern libraries are the tool to empower the scholars. Present academic societies are highly influenced by information and communication technology applications. The scholars are also enjoying this environment and speed of contents delivery.

References

Sundararajan, N. 2015. Digitization of higher education in India: Making the dream reality changing landscape of higher education. *University News*, 53(47), 10-21.

http://shodhganga.inflibnet.ac.in/ (retrieved on August 17, 2017).

http://nlist.inflibnet.ac.in/ (retrieved on August 17, 2017).

22

PG College Librarians in the 21st Century: Changing Roles and Responsibilities

P.C. Meena

ABSTRACT

This chapter describes the librarian's responsibilities in the 21st century. It deals with how the conventional libraries are in the path of change due to various reasons and most striking one is impact of ICT. Further, it describes in this changing environment about the roles and responsibilities of library professionals.

Keywords: *Librarians; Roles and Responsibilities; ICT.*

Introduction

Information scenario keeps changing with the development of national and global information infrastructure. The 'Information Technology' Revolution has brought a huge impact upon the society and economy activities. Information has become a significant component of world economic activity and being recognized as a major economic resource. Harker (1996) claimed that a tidal wave of change is headed towards the telecommunication industry, and it will ultimately transform the economic, social and political environment for nearly every person in the world. This change has been referred to as the 3T Wave, 'The Information Revolution' by Alvin Toffler, and the 'InfoCosm' by Anderson Consulting and 'Convergence' by Gemini Consulting. Keiser (1992) added that technological advancements in telecommunications allowed information users to exchange information more freely and globally. Living standards have been raised and the problems of everyday living eased considerably. Much of the change is being brought by technological innovation and the information revolution—the convergence of computing, communication and information. Organizations that acknowledge and prepare for this revolution will emerge as winners.

Librarianship is now at crossroads. The avalanche of document and information has posed serious problems to the traditional methods of organizing libraries and information centers. Actually, these methods are fast crumbling down. New methods of handling documents and information have been thought out in the West and librarians in the United States of America are already in the dawn of the paperless society. In Japan, which has gone several steps further, than the developed countries of the West, the home computer has become a normal feature. Probably, in the 21st century, there will be no need for large collections of books, or for huge, imposing buildings to house such collections. It would also not be necessary to appoint a fleet of professional staff to look after such libraries. Everybody concerned—the librarians and the information scientists, the readers and the research workers—would have to stay at their homes and operate their computer terminals to supply the information required or to receive the information needed (Deshpande, 1986).

Impact of Technology on Library Services

In academic environment, library is a place of intellectual stimulation and knowledge centre. It holds thousands of results of past research studies providing scope for further research. Until 1980s, the information seekers were greatly dependent on print resources, and libraries were unique places for provision of such information. The past two decades have seen demand for new patterns of scholarly information. These technological advancements have made significant impact on the growth of knowledge and unlocking of human potential. In library environment, the impact is clearly visible on information resources services and people. Some of the notable impacts have been illustrated in the following:

Product

- **Changing document collections:** In the past, the word collection referred mostly to the print materials. Today a library collection goes beyond the print materials and includes the CD-ROMs, audio-video cassettes, e-books, e-journals also;
- **The storage media:** The traditional paper as medium of storage is getting replaced with electronic media such as tapes, CDs/DVDs, and Web pages;
- **Format:** The traditional text format is being enriched by graphics and voice.

Functions

Automation of library in-house operations: Various in-house operations in the library like book acquisitions, processing, and circulations, maintenance, reminders and serials management are repetitive in nature. The need for automation is repetitive in nature. The need for automation arises as to reduce the effort and time required for these jobs. In addition to these, there are occasional functions like preparation of statistical reports. Computers are used in creating databases of information to form a basis for retrieving the relevant information when required by the user. The statistical reports related to transactions budget expenditures and other key issues can be generated with ease.

Resource Sharing: The ICT has helped in establishing networking. The library networking and resource sharing is more often carried out effectively through Internet and Intranet. Library networks have expanded the limitation of the scope of resource sharing from inter-library loan and document supply to sharing materials, functions, services and expertise.

Reprography: The invention and entry of reprographic or duplication techniques into the portals of libraries made many things easier for libraries as well as the readers. This helped the readers to get the copies of the documents and to reproduce rare/ torn out books, this also helps to save the library budget spent on purchase of back issues of journals or reprints, to preserve the handwritten manuscripts.

Communication: The advent of communication technology has revolutionized the activities of library and information system. Today, the internet provides efficient means of communication and Libraries/librarians are using it extensively to communicate with vendors of library products and services, scholars, researchers and users via email.

The Internet technology: Gave birth to another powerful media called e-discussion forums. These forums connect people for networking, exchange the information and solutions to problems and navigate documents all over the world.

Search engines and instant message: The emergence of free search engines like Google, yahoo and MSN, do provide wide scope for information search across the globe and connects many people instantly.

Quality of service: Application of information technology has contributed immensely for the improvement in provision of quick and quality services through which the libraries try to achieve customers' satisfaction.

People-Customers/Users

Choice of sources: The technology has enabled the users to have multiple sources of information such as Internet, commercial information service providers. As a result, the library is not the only source of information provision for information seekers.

Death of distance: The emergence of the Internet has paved the way for access to global information trespassing all geographical barriers.

Diminishing time-zones: The present day information seekers can obtain the information overcoming the time barriers.

Remote access: Today, information seekers can access the worldwide information across the globe through their desktops without any time limitations (24 × 7 × 365 days).

Basic skills: Unlike in past, the current users need to possess basic technical skills to access the information in electronic media.

On line search: Another impact is to access variety of commercial and non-commercial information sources including bibliographic and full text databases, tables of contents of primary journals, electronic and online journals, books and newsletter, library catalogues and Open Public Access Catalogue (OPAC), graphics data bases etc. Now through network one can access a remote computer. And use it interactively as if the local computer were a terminal of that host machine. Automatic indexing, Selective Dissemination of Information (SDI) and Current Awareness Service (CAS) activities are added services to the IT based library Services.

People-Staff

Duties and Responsibilities of the Library Professionals:

In this age of information technology the duties of library professionals have changed. Earlier the librarians were considered as the custodian of books or information. The changing environment forces the librarian to restructure their library to suit the requirements of their customers. Today, the libraries require a dynamic librarian, who is ready to accept the changes and challenges. Thomas Frey (2005), Executive Director of the DaVinci Institute, Colorado traced 10 key changing trends like (i) communication systems, (ii) replacement of existing technology by new one, (iii) size of storage device, (iv) search technology, (v) time compression of readers, (vi) verbal society, (vii) demand for global information, (viii) global systems, (ix) transition from product economy to experience economy, and (x) library as cultural centre that are affecting the development of the next generation library.

THE 'CHANGE'

Forces for Change

Computer technologies are a major force that have affected all concerned professionals in the value added information chain including libraries and information professionals. Not only the world becoming an interconnected global community, it has changed and shifted the fundamental roles, paradigms and organizational culture of libraries and information professionals as well. Opportunities have never been better for the librarian in a non-traditional setting. The Internet and cutting-edge information technology have created new jobs which demand new skills. The image of the profession, if not more positive than before, is certainly changing as new jobs are emerging. Now is the time for profession to show the rest of the world that what skills its members possess and how those skills mesh with the emerging job requirements. Change is running rampant in libraries with technology as the driving force. From recent writings and literatures, the paradigm shifts for libraries and information professionals can be seen as indicated in tables 1 and 2 that is from the traditional setting to an electronic era. Information professionals as the resource person in the libraries too, have shifted their activities and roles due to these changes. Table 2 indicates the trend of paradigm shifts for the information professionals from the traditional roles to a new role.

Why the Need to 'Change'?

'Change' is the only constraint, facing libraries and information professionals in the 21st century. Academic libraries and especially, PG college libraries have to change and expand their horizons for the following reasons:

(a) Positioning the library as leading players in the information industry and major providers of information services using the latest and advanced IT.

(b) Competitive with other information providers, including information brokers and networks because of the marked increase in user expectation.

(c) The techno-revolution is recreating the workplace and academic libraries as organizations are not immune for its impact.

(d) Shift in focus and it is vital that the information age must now give way to the communication age (Burrus, 1993).

(e) The concept of the library as a warehouse of information has lost validity.

(f) Enhance skills in leadership, business relationships and technology through change opportunities.

Table 1: Paradigm Shift for Libraries

Library before Electronic Era	Library in Electronic Era
Printed with fixed, permanent, collections	Electronic formatted text
Go to the library	Library at the door steps
Own collection and museum of distributed collections	Virtual collections and information resources
Information confined with in the library	Anywhere
Static library facilities with fixed stacks	Dynamic without stacks
Hierarchical organizational structure	Non-hierarchical organizational structure
Management style—Rank and File	Electronic file formats
Standard reference services	Online reference services
Free library services	Free and fee-based library services
Small scale budgets	Need large scale budgets
Need large physical space	Less space required

Table 2: Shift in Roles for Information Professionals

Traditional Roles	New Roles
Job designation: Librarian	Information manager, System Administrator
Name of Profession: Library Science	Information Science and Technology
Custodian of books and keeper of knowledge	Information and knowledge dissemination
Preoccupation with collections	Preoccupation with information
Collection maintenance and custodial tasks	Information Resource Management

Roles and Responsibilities of Librarians

Positions and Duties: Specific duties vary depending on the size and type of library. Olivia Crosby described librarians as 'Information experts in the information age'. Responsibilities of librarians as stated in Wikipedia are as follows:

Researching topics of interest for their constituencies:

- Referring patrons to other community organizations and government offices
- Suggesting appropriate books ('readers' advisory') for children of different reading levels, and recommending novels for recreational reading

- Facilitating and promoting reading clubs
- Developing programs for library users of all ages and backgrounds
- Managing access to electronic information resources
- Building collections to respond to changing community needs or demands
- Creating pathfinders
- Writing grants to gain funding for expanded program or collections
- Digitising collections for online access
- Answering incoming reference questions via telephone, postal mail, email, fax and chat
- Making and enforcing computer appointments on the public access Internet computers (Wikipedia).

The Changing Role of Librarian

Information Technology is rapidly changing the whole world creating new challenges and opportunities. Library and Information Service (LIS) profession is one of the most challenging professions in the knowledge society, combining expertise in information management with the Information and Communication Technology (ICT) competencies.

The ICT has tremendous impact on library operation, resource, services, staff and users. The LIS professionals are confronting challenging dynamic technological environment demanding the extensive and effective utilization of ICT in order to survive and meet the changing complex information needs of user community. The change is the law of nature.

The ICT is driving force of change in library. Change is inevitable for the survival and success of any library in the changing technological world. The LIS professionals must develop expert technological competencies required to make best use of the opportunities, the ICT offers in order to provide a gateway access to wide range and variety of information resources and services.

New Challenges for Library and Information Science Professionals

The major challenges for library and information science professionals as stated by (Ramana, 2006) are as followings:

- Information Explosion
- The ICT Revolution
- Explosive growth and usage of Web resources
- Dwindling library budgets
- Escalating cost of printed documents
- Intensive use of digital resources
- Heightened level of users' expectations
- Interactive virtual learning environment
- Evolution of virtual educational in institutions
- Changing nature and number of information resources
- New patterns of scholarly publishing and communication
- Development of digital, virtual and hybrid libraries
- Online bookshops and information services.

These challenges have called for reorientation, re-engineering, transformation and great changes in the information environment, library functions and the roles of library and information service professionals.

Conclusion

Libraries need to change quite dramatically to modernize almost every aspect of their operations, information resources and services in order to meet the rising users' expectations. As the world advances, the library must also evolve and redesign their activities in order to deliver highly qualitative, need-based and value-added services according to the expectations of today's library users. The change is inevitable for the survival and success of any library in the changing technological world. The LIS professionals must develop expert technological competencies required to make best use of the opportunities.

References

Abrahamson, E. 2000. Change without pain, *Harvard Business Review*, 28(5), 23-29.

Armstrong, M. 1988. A Handbook of Personnel Management Practice. 3rd ed. London: Kogan, p. 712.

Brophy, P. 2001. The library in the twenty-first century: New services for the information age. London: Library Association Publishing, pp. 10-11.

Burrus, D. 1993. Techno trends, Harper Business, United States of America.

Chad, K. and Paul, M. 2005. 'Do Libraries Matter? The rise of Library 2.0'. A White Paper, pp. 1-11. Nov. www.talis.com. Accesssed on 20.12.2005.

Collins, E. 1984. Taking hold of change. *Harvard Business Review*. May-June.

Daft, R.L. 1992. Organization Theory and Designi., Saint Paul, MN: West

Deshpande, K.S. 1986. Problems of Indian editors of Library Science Journals: Case Study, (Edited by B. Guha). In The Library and Information Science Horizon, A collection of essays in honour of Dr. A.V. Kamath, presented by the Bombay Science Librarians' Association. (BOSLA). pp. 409-22, New Delhi: Allied Publishers Private Limited.

Dowlin, K.E. 1984. *The Electronic Library*. New York: Neal-Schuman Publishers, p. 199.

Drucker, P.F. 1964. The big power of little ideas. *Harvard Business Review*, Vol. 42, May, pp. 6-8.

Duck, J.D. 1998. Managing change; The art of Balancing. Boston: Harvard Business School Publisher.

Durcker, P.F. 1979. *The Practice of Management*. Pan Books Ltd., London.

Etim, S.O. 2002. Change management and intelligence activities in the Nigerian banking industry. *Union Digest*, 7(1 & 2), 50-63.

Federal Librarians in the 21st century: Changing roles in the electronic age : Summary report on Conference Proceeding (September 15, 1993). Library of Congress. http:/www.Loc.gov/falice/21cent html. Accessed on 22.12.2005.

Harker, R.A. 1996. AFRICON, IEEE AFRICON 4th Volume: 1, Pretoria, South Africa.

Hofmann, U. 1995. Developing a strategic planning framework for information technologies for libraries. OCLC Systems and Services, Vol. 11, No. 4, pp. 22-32.

Irene, E. McDermott. 2006. The librarian's Internet survival guide: Strategies for the high-tech reference desk, Ed. Barbara E. Quint, Foreword by Joseph Janes, pp. 1-2, *Information Today.*

Keiser, B. 1992. Kaiser memo to: Don Graham...invitation to attend an Apple-organized conference on the future of "multimedia"—computers, telecommunications. Accessed from recovering journalist. typepad.com/files/Kaiser-memo.pdf.

Khosrowpour. 1990. *Managing change: The art of balancing*. Boston: Harvard Business School Publisher.

King, W. 2006. Role of information technology in growth of business. Source: http://EzineArticles.com/?expert=William King.

Malhotra, Y. 1993. Role of information technology in managing organizational change and organizational interdependence [WWW document]. URL http://www.brint.com/papers/change/

McKinzie, S. 2002. 'For Ethical Reference, Pare the Paraprofessionals'. *American Libraries*, October, Vol. 33, No. 9, p. 42.

Mullins, V. Ferguson, S. and Houghton, J. 2000. INF 100. The Information Society and Future of Library and Information Services: Study guide, Charles Sturt University, Wagga. p. 5.

Olivia, C. 2000. Librarians: Information Experts in the Information Age. *Occupational Outlook Quarterly*, Winter. http://stats.bls.gov/opub/ooq/2000/winter/contents.htm.

Paper. Talis.com Accessed on October 28, 2014.

Ramana, V.P. 2006. The changing role of librarian in a challenging dynamic Web environment. 4th International Convention CALIBER-2006, Gulbarga, 2-4 February. INFLIBNET Centre.

Shashi, N. 2002. Professional competencies for special librarians of the 21st century. http://144.16.72.189/ is 206/ assign-2002/shashi-competency-professional.doc

Tennant, R. 1998. Strategies for building 21st century libraries and librarians. In Robots of know boats: The wider automation agenda. Proceedings of the Victorian Association for Library Automation 9th Biennial Conference, January 28-30, VALA, pp. 503-507.

The DaVinci Institute, Inc. Download from http://www.davinciinstitute.com/page.php?ID=120.

Theja, K.A. and De Silva W.R.G. 2007. Library automation: Strategies for library human resource management. *Journal of the University Librarians*, Vol. 11, p. 106.

Wikipedia http://si.wikipedia.org/wiki

Zohar, D. 1997. *Rewiring the corporate brain*. San Francisco: Berret-Koehler.

23

Maintenance of Public Relations in Academic Libraries

P. Srinivasulu

ABSTRACT

The library is a service oriented organization and supports the entire academic activities in an educational campus. The role of librarian is continuing to evolve with the adoption of new technologies. To achieve best possible results of library usage, the librarian needs to maintain the public relation with the library users, administrators, service providers and vendors. This chapter highlights the public relation issues in libraries, discussed the public relation tools used in the libraries, Public relations practice in the regular university on campus and off campus.

Keywords: *Public Relations; Public Relations-Academic Librarian.*

Introduction

The importance of public relation activities cannot be overlooked in any library, especially in academic libraries. The academic library activity, directly or indirectly, is an act of public relations, much as it is done to promote the library image and usage. The librarian is overall part of the library professionals working in each and every library to fulfil the required services of the library successful. The librarian is the intermediary between the users and the library resources and services. The library or library professionals can easily know what the users need and what the library has, therefore, the role of the public relations activities cannot be overstated. All the library professionals should be involved in public relations activities, those library professionals whose work is directly related with the users perform more of public relations activities than the others, for example the librarian and the reference librarian.

Meaning Public Relations: The public relations of libraries means the act of process of the library into cordial and understanding relationship with all the users of the community. It means average user's understanding of library functions, policies and procedure, the extent and warmth of the user's community good will toward the library, and its appreciation for the quality and morale of the library's staff and services.

What is Public Relations: The public relations is an activity geared towards human relationships to enhance good services. Since the library serves human beings, so it includes the role played by the librarian and the role played by the library professionals of any organization.

Aims: The aim of the library public relations is to build up public belief, active, forward looking, quickly responsive to users demands, interested in progressive methods and economy, operated by devoted and highly skilled staff and busy in helping more user's in every category. Public relation programme is not to describe services and materials; it has to explain library objectives, problems, plans, projects, personnel, standards and accomplishments.

Definitions: According to Angoff (1973) PR is defined "as a communication technique" or a "kind of advertising or publishing activities."

According to World Bank Encyclopaedia (2002), "Public relations are an activity aimed at increasing communication and understanding between an organization or individual and one or more groups called publics."

According to M. Crozier, the term "Public relations has an overall application and refers to a function. It comes to us from the United States, and often stands for all the methods used to gain the sympathy and goodwill of the outside world".

According to the international Public Relations Association "Public relations is a management function where by a public or private body seeks to secure and keep the understanding, sympathy and co-operation of those with whom it has, or may have, dealings."

Objectives: Broadly speaking, the objectives of the library public relations programme are:

- To create library consciousness among the people of the community,
- To spotlight the existence of libraries, where they are located, what do they contain, and to identify the services they can render to help people in their informal self-education,
- To make constructive use of their leisure hours,
- To become good citizens,
- To help people remain well-informed,
- To appreciate the values of democracy, and
- To increase their theoretical knowledge of their vocations.

Functions of the Librarian

- The librarian co ordinates the services of the library at the service point, wherever the users request attending, through the library assistants, discharges its duties by serving users either by helping them searching articles or titles on shelves or by charging out books for a period of time.
- The librarian acts as an intermediary between the library and the users, co-ordinating services and making them available to users.
- The librarian disseminates the already acquired information to serve users.
- The librarian links the users with the information available in the library, or links the information with the users through selective dissemination of information and current awareness services.

The Tools of PRs in the Libraries

- Library location labels
- Catalogues
- Shelf arrangement and self-guides exhibitions
- Media talks

- Notice boards for both staff and students
- Bulletin boards
- Suggestion boxes
- Public information desks
- Online chatting
- Instant messaging
- Maintaining Library blogs
- Latest tools like Watts app, face book, etc.

Public Relations: International Bodies: The international bodies like UNESCO, IFLA and FID have played a vital role in projecting library image on international level.

UNESCO has been playing a vital role in the development of libraries in many parts of the world. Although UNESCO is concerned with all kinds of libraries but it has paid special attention for the development of public libraries in those countries which have not been fortunate enough to have them.

IFLA has influenced the march of librarianship but in a different way. It operates section for national and university libraries, for public libraries, for special libraries, for parliamentary libraries and administrative libraries. There are also subsections working for libraries in hospitals, children, astronomical and geographical libraries.

IFLA committees perform work relating to library education, rare books, periodicals, statistics and library buildings, etc.

FID has made great contributions to spread the latest developments in documentation, information science and UDC throughout the world.

Public Relations: National Bodies

The national library association like ALA (USA), Library Association (London), Indian Library Association (India) have recognised image at international level. They promote the librarians to participate in international conferences/workshops/seminars by conducting themselves, by establishing fellowships for librarians from developing countries and arranging the scholars for visiting libraries in their respective countries.

At the national level, the working government at national, state assemblies and local level are playing a vital role in departmental libraries. They give financial assistance directly and indirectly for the maintenance and development of academic libraries.

Public Relation on the University Campus: The university governing bodies like Vice-Chancellors, Faculty, Library Committees and also Students must be kept informed about library's needs and services.

Vice-Chancellor: The librarian has to educate Vice-Chancellor about library's progress and problems. If the library is poorly or brilliantly organized, the Vice-Chancellor will come to know about it from the faculty, library committee, students or even the alumni. But if the librarian requires new equipment for initiating new services, he must keep the Vice-Chancellor informed.

The Vice-Chancellor is being informed about

- Book funds,
- Integrating the library with instruction, teaching and extension programmes,
- The library costs involved for starting new courses,
- Building's expansion for accommodating new acquisition, and new equipments,
- New activities like the computer application to libraries which call for modifications or extension of buildings that requires unusual expenditure of funds,
- The advantages and disadvantages of decentralising collection and services,
- The money earmarked for the purchase of special and rare collections,
- The quality of stall and costs involved to operate a first rate library, and
- The aspiration of staff for recognition and appropriate faculty status, etc.

The librarian should be careful to present all sides of his recommendations and problems to enable the vice-chancellor to give whole-hearted support.

Library Committee: The possible way for the librarian to interpret his services and resources is through the library committees. Such committees should be advisory and consultative. The advisory committee can be immensely helpful in promoting the cause of library; the advisory function should be taken to mean that the teaching faculty advise the library of its wishes and requirements through its representatives on the committee. Its consultative factions should be interpreted as the university librarian consulting the teaching faculty through the committee.

Faculty: The librarian must work in close cooperation with the faculty for projecting the library image in the university and among students. Since, faculty and students are the primary users of a university library, their needs must be of paramount importance to the library in setting goals.

Public Relations off the University Campus: The off campus groups towards the public relation programme of the university library may be directed are alumni, friends of the library and professional associations and organizations.

Alumni: The alumnus is given a special status; he/she should always be invited for short periods of time. Alumni who live near the university may make use of its library directly, other may seek loans by mail, they may also ask for reference and bibliographical services by online. The librarian is interested to build the library services through alumni assistance; he can seek their help in proper mechanism.

The librarian may organize exhibition for alumni day and can meet as many alumni as possible and inform about the library services and its needs. The outstanding acquisition of books, book gift, special services, and new likely to be of interest to the alumni.

Friends of the Library: Friends look upon the library as an informational and cultural force in the community, as a source of inspiration and as a tool to promote individual, civil, and national development. Friend's organizations are established for promoting and understanding the library, its limitations, its services, its physical facilities, and its resources. More specifically, they may and frequently do promote and encourage gifts to the library either in kind or cash.

Participation of librarian in professional association/ organizations: Wilson and Tauber enumerate four groups of organizations, with which the university librarian has at one time or another, worked. These are:

- Library association—local, state, regional, national, and international
- Educational associations
- Government offices and departments
- Educational foundations and societies
- The types of activities of these organizations which appeal most to the librarians include the following:
- The development of international cultural relations
- The compilation and publication of major catalogues and union lists
- The establishment of regional union catalogues and bibliographical centres
- The description of the holdings of individual libraries and groups of libraries
- Improvement of college and university book collections
- The improvement and support of education for librarianship
- The development of physical facilities for the photographic reproduction of materials
- The reduction of costs of library technical operations
- The re-classification and re-cataloguing of library collections
- The study of specific aid for learning, and
- The accomplishment of other undertakings all of which are intended to contribute to the promotion of research and the advancement of scholarship and librarianship.

The participation in professional meetings of the state or the national associations or the learned bodies may stimulate and refresh the participants and they may return home with new experience, new vision, new ideas and new methods to try with, which ultimately improve services having their impact on educational role of the library. Confident and enthusiastic staff members, receptive to nascent professional thought and latest techniques of operating libraries and disseminating information, gain the confidence and respect of their teaching colleagues.

Media Used for Public Relation Work: Usually, the librarian use the following media in their public relation work to interpret the services of the library to the below mentioned groups:

Annual reports: The annual report of the library is a written document submitted by the librarian to keep his management fully and effectively informed on the aspects of library services, achievements or regress along with plausible reasons of his short-comings to clarify and reinforce the library's request for support.

The following topics are usually included in annual reports:

- The state and growth of the collections
- Services to the readers
- Statistics of the preparation units
- Personnel matters, including activities of staff members
- Information regarding income and expenditure
- Descriptions of improvements made in the buildings or of equipment added
- Special problems of administration and organization
- Description of efforts to improve the services of the library
- Notes of special progress
- Work of the separate departments for divisions, and
- Recommendation for the future.

Library surveys: The basic purpose of library survey is to explore. The survey report can form a good public relations document in itself. But more than that, it can offer a solid foundation for any future public relation policy. Library which has been critically and objectively examined in respect of its services, book collections, staff, faculty attitudes and teaching methods, the acquisition policy, financial and administrative support, building programmes, operations in the cataloguing, binding, reference, technical or circulation departments, special services, major obstacles to its developments, deserves credit for shaking itself out of lethargy.

Handbook: The small handbooks are a valuable device to instruct and assist the students to help them. Sometimes, a separate handbook is prepared for the faculty.

The handbooks should be concise, well-arranged and written in simple and clear style. The student library handbook contains a mine of current facts.

- Diagrammatically representation of the main service floor
- The location of principal collections and service points
- The location and arrangement of books, the method of charging and discharging books
- The rules and regulations of the library
- The library collections and its special services
- Description of library catalogue and detailed instructions to use it by means of sample card and brief notes, tells what a call slip is and how it should be filled out, directs the students to books-stacks and the particular section indicated by the call number. Similarly, directions are given about the use and methods of obtaining periodicals, newspapers and government publications.

Printed Catalogue: Printing is an important means for publishing library contents. It may include total holdings of the central as well as branch libraries or may be restricted to special collections of the library. The printed catalogue should be accurate, well-indexed, well-designed and well-printed. The printed catalogues are quite useful in the library's public relations programme.

Library Bulletin: The library bulletin helps to increase the usefulness of the library. By means of brief book lists, it encourages the use of books for general and recreational reading.

News Sheets: Some of the libraries which cannot afford to produce costly library bulletins may resort to the issue of printed or mimeographed or typed handbills and now's-sheets.

Press: The librarians who cannot even afford to produce new-sheets, may profitably sue the local press for disseminating information over to users.

Posters and Bulletin Boards: The librarians use posters and bulletin boards to stimulate people's interest in special resources and services, to invite attention to selected books on a particular topic, to present short, graphic summaries of important national local news, and to announce programmes and lectures.

Posters, pictures, book jackets, maps, slogans, notes on special days, authors, and events, constitute the display material for the bulletin board.

Personal Talk: Direct personal talk is the simplest and the least expensive method of publicity. It can convert non-users into regular users of the library. The university and college librarians are expected to talk about libraries to new entrants, students, organizations, faculty members, and often to outside bodies as well.

Public Relation on Air: The librarians are using the Radio/TV for publishing their services. If Radio/TV talk is to be given live, librarian must be conscious that each item is brief and effectively phrased, revolves around specific subjects.

National Library Weeks: The organization of material library week is one of the most ambitions means of library public relations work. This is a cooperative method of publicity including book-seller, publishers, authors and librarians. It must have a theme, a symbol, and slogan, a stylized recognizable printed publicity.

Children Book Weeks: The children's book weeks have been an important element of library public relations work. The programme must be planned carefully. The children love to meet authors and book illustrators whose names are known to them. The librarian should also arrange talks of known authors in children's world.

Visiting Groups: Another important form of public relations programmes is visiting groups to the library—whether comprising of international delegations or of groups from conferences or from other local authorities or groups of the students. The librarian must give a careful thought for planning such a visit as each individual member of the visiting group takes back with its impression about the library in every aspect.

Conclusion

The continuous public relations work is necessary. Repetition builds reputation. The Librarian should adopt the public relation skills to encourage the users to properly utilise the services and resources. The long time relationship with the public makes the librarian in comfortable zone to market the entire library resources and services properly. Hence, the library is a service oriented organization.

References

Aitufe, T.A. 1993. Public relations in academic libraries. *Library Review*. 42(2), 39-45.

Babafemi, Grace Olabisi. 2002. Public Relations activities in an academic Library: the roles of the Circulation Librarian. *Library Review*. 5(9), 464-68.

Bloomberg, M. 1981. Introduction to public services for library technicians. 3rd ed., Libraries Unlimited Inc., Englewood. Co. pp. 284-85.

Chai, Y. 1996. *Review of library public relations studies*. Library and information service, No. 2.

Cosette, K. 1974. *Problems in library public relations*. R.R. Bowker & Co., New York.

Harrison, K.C. 1973. Public relations for libraries. Grafton Books, Deutsch.

http://article.sapub.org/10.5923.j.library.20120102.04.html

Israel, Odede. 2012. "Public relations activities in an academic library: the roles of the reference librarian." *International Journal of Library Science*, 1(2), pp. 38-42.

Khanna, J.K. 2008. "Advances in Library Administration." Y.K. Publishers, Agra, pp. 1-464.

World Book. 2002. "World book encyclopedia." Vol. 15 Part 3, World Book Inc., Scott Fetzer Co., Chicago, IL, p. 868.

24

Sustainability Practices for Green Library as Future Transformation of Libraries

Umesh Sharma and Prashant Goswami

ABSTRACT

This chapter deals with that how the library can also play some different role to educate the society for other social issues like saving the environment. This paper is based on the primary theory of the concept "Green Library". It also includes the other aspects of the term with some major steps to be taken towards making a conventional library—Green Library.

Keywords: *Green Library; Environment; Green Building; Sustainable; Indoor Environment.*

Introduction

Libraries are the learning centers for people of all ages. Libraries are not only repositories of knowledge, but are also important information resources for raising awareness about social issues like environment, education and other related topics. Green library is the new emerging field in LIS education. History describes its emergence in 1970s. Green libraries educate the public about environmental issues through their collections, sustainable and environment friendly facilities, and through other programs. Among other things, green libraries maximize the effects of natural sunlight and natural air flow; green libraries are thoughtfully designed while taking into account site selection to structural design, energy use, materials used and human health effects and many more.

Global warming is one of the reasons for the emergence of Green library concept. Global warming is the term used to describe a gradual increase in the average temperature of the Earth's atmosphere. As a part of society, it is duty of library to participate and contribute in social responsibility. This contribution can be termed as "Library Social Responsibility".

What is Green Library?

A Green library encompasses not only design and refurbishment of library buildings, but also includes structure design efficiency, energy efficiency, water efficiency, materials selection, indoor environmental quality operations and maintenance, and waste and toxics reduction. This may improve day-to-day operations and procedures of the library, as well as educating the community about responsible environmental practices.

Why Green for Library?

"Green" is not only the term but it is an idea that is not emerged for application only but this is perceptible which can be felt. This has an active impact on the society. As library is the thing that is made by the society for society welfare. So it is not only the vivid concept but also the responsibility of library towards it society, that is why library is called "growing organism". Undoubtedly, Green is the demand of the time but it is not able. "Green" does not belong to the area of civil and architecture only. This belongs to the society also, and being a part of the society, library should also contribute to its extent.

On the other hand, library is a not profit organization. Application of Green to the library will definitely save its wealth too in long-term.

What is the Present Scenario about Library Building?

Currently, most of the library buildings in India are traditional buildings. Still the education community is not serious about this issue. Probably following may be the myths behind it:

- Green/sustainable buildings cost much more than conventional buildings.

- It is just another fed and therefore not, particularly important.
- Green buildings are often unattractive or ugly and lack the aesthetic quality of conventional buildings.
- Green building is essentially about eco-friendly materials selection.
- Green building does not provide the comfort levels.
- Green building products are often difficult to find.
- Green building uses traditional tools and techniques and is not cutting-edge technology.
- Green building products don't work as well as traditional ones.
- Building green is too difficult and complicated.
- It is difficult or not possible to convert existing conventional library building into energy efficient buildings.
- Building green requires signing up for a green program or third-party certification.

Going green is an all-or-nothing proposition and many more.

For all the above myths, it can be said that there are more possibilities, techniques and materials available that can prove these kind of myths, wrong.

The building sector has the potential to make a huge impact on environment either in positive or negative manner. A study says that typically green buildings use around 30% less energy, and remit 33% less greenhouse gases than traditional buildings.

Many reports also state that environmental designs should be to create buildings and neighbourhoods that benefit the community, use less energy & water, produce no waste in operation or construction, and are made of materials that are derived from sustainable sources. Whilst this may be difficult to achieve in practice, this aim should be the theoretical goal for sustainable opportunities that are considered in any project.

Any green buildings should include aspects of Environmentally Sustainable Design (ESD) principles, which are:

- Reducing energy consumption and cost
- Providing a natural environment for people
- Passive and active ventilation, heating and cooling
- Natural lighting
- Reducing heat in summer
- Reduction in water usage.

Responsibilities that can be redeemed by the Library for going Green:

Reducing Energy Consumption: Library can achieve a reduction in energy consumption and costs by implementing a number of different strategies ranging from renewable energy sources to energy efficient lighting and climate control systems.

These are smarter and cleaner ways available for meeting the energy needs of a building. This can be achieved through some changes in the existing building structure and also via using solar. Solar power generates power by converting sunlight into electricity. Energy produced, can power fixtures and appliances in a building. Solar panels require a significant upfront cost, but once installed they need little maintenance and can last for up to twenty years. Excess energy can be fed into the main electricity grid or into a storage system.

Renewable energy systems reduce greenhouse emissions, decrease demand on conventional energy resources and are becoming more cost effective in the long-term.

Indoor Environment Quality: Following principles and systematic library building designs can achieve efficient and sustainable indoor environment quality. A sustainable design should incorporate the following:

- Try to increase dependency on daylight and more use of energy efficient light fittings.
- High quality windows glasses can prevent ultraviolet rays, heat gain and unwanted sound from the out.
- Passive solar heating will keep summer sun out and letting the winter sun in.
- Passive cooling may achieve natural cooling during summer and minimizing energy use for cooling.

- High quality insulation throughout the building will minimizes heat loss and heat gain through walls, roofs and floors.
- Airtight enveloped building design can be a boon for new library buildings.
- Energy efficient cooling and heating systems, such as in-floor systems which don't require air to be cooled as much and therefore reduce energy consumption.
- Night purge systems to effectively cool buildings overnight during the warmer months to reduce the reliance on air conditioning systems.
- The use of rooftop gardens, which will absorb heat from direct sunlight on the roof, and reduce reliance on mechanical air conditioning, whilst also removing CO_2 from the air.

Water Saving: The following ideas can be implemented to reduce water consumption:

- Harvest enough rainwater.
- Once the harvesting system installed and water runoff increases—this runoff can be stored in water tanks, which can be used for landscaping or toilets.
- Tanks that are underground or in-ground are preferred for water storage.
- The use of mulch on garden beds keeps the soil moist and minimizes water loss from the soil and reduces the need for watering.
- The use of automatic or sensor taps and dual flush toilets will dramatically reduce water consumption in the facilities.
- Waterless urinals can dramatically decrease water usage in bathrooms.
- Efficient fixtures and fittings such as flow regulators or aerators on taps.
- Avoid leaks wherever possible and aim to have them fixed as soon as they are noticed.

Operational Activities Reduce, Reuse, Recycle: These are terms synonymous with sustainable living, when it comes to reducing a business impact on the environment. But there is far more to sustainable practices than just these three concepts. It's important for libraries to start "thinking outside the box" in terms of truly sustainable practices. Ensuring initiatives are embraced and changing the mindset of the users and the staff alike are essential steps in the process of moving to a sustainable library.

Below is a list of initiatives that libraries can incorporate to ensure they operate more sustainably. Some libraries will be able to adopt all, or most of these ideas, however, some will be able to adopt only a limited number of them, depend upon budgetary constraints. It is important to recognize that some of these initiatives will, in fact, reduce a library's operating costs:

- Signage in staffing areas i.e. "Please turns off lights when leaving room." More smart lightning systems are available today i.e. sensitive light system, movement-sensitive light system, energy-efficient light systems etc.
- Energy efficient heating/cooling should be used. This saves more energy and cost.
- Invest in green IT solutions—e.g. energy efficient servers, printers, photocopiers, computers, screens, programs.
- try to recycle e-waste or start using such material that can be recycled.
- Increase the use of one-sided used paper. And recycle the both side used paper putting instead of in dustbin.
- Waste bins in every area of the library for rubbish, paper products, recyclables (different color for different functions).
- A waste audit system can be used as a starting point for measuring the library's waste and can reduce misuse.
- Greater reliance on e-resources to reduce paper production and waste in monograph production.
- Resource sharing such as Inter Library Loan to reduce the number of items required.

- More use of electronic media for information sharing instead of use of papers, etc.
- Giving facility for remote access systems, video conferencing, etc. also will help library in going green. This will also reduce fuel/energy cost to reach library in many cases.
- Implementation of recognition system for best efforts made.

Many operational procedures and practices are "entrenched" in the library industry. It is imperative that library management ensure that all staff is included in the planning, implementation and management of the new policies. This will ensure staff to feel that they are included and have some ownership of the changes involved in moving towards a more sustainable way of operating.

Aside from being intrinsically valuable, green public building projects can be excellent vehicles for initiating broader community conversations about sustainability.

Libraries are traditional places associated with learning and R&D, so it is fitting that "green" libraries use their buildings to demonstrate green technologies and practices. Libraries can show their patrons how these practices can be applied at home, work and in the community.

Public libraries are well positioned in their communities to deliver education programs about environmental sustainability. Libraries can use a variety of methods to educate the community about responsible environmental practices. Some of these methods can include:

Resources: Libraries can provide access to a range of resources including books, magazines, DVDs and energy kits. Inform and educate the community and create awareness of environmental issues. It also aims to encourage participation in preserving the local environment.

In-Library Displays: A library that has successfully implemented green practices and/or sustainable building design can create displays within the library that help to educate the public about the sustainable strategies employed and their positive impact on the environment. The use of monitors to display slideshows featuring the building project from start to finish, including commentary on ESD features can help to create interest and give a good background on the project and its key goals and objectives. Communication and transparency is an essential element of community education. By highlighting the key ESD features of the building, including recycling and re-use of materials from a demolished site, libraries are demonstrating sound sustainability practices and encouraging the community to think about ways that they can do the same. It also fosters a sense of community satisfaction: patrons like to know that their rates are being put to good use. Book displays are also an excellent way of educating the community on sustainability. Creative, attractive displays featuring items from the collection such as building green homes, water and energy saving, and recycling create interest and awareness about environmental issues.

Energy Dashboards: Other initiatives include monitors within the building displaying the performance of the building using programs such as "e-Gauge MySmartCTI" software. This technology can be used within the library and on the library's website. This software is a visual, practical way of educating the community on energy efficiency, and demonstrates the effects that the ESD features are having on the actual energy consumption of the building. This software has the capacity to include sustainability tips as well as detailed information about the library's green features.

Apart from the above there may be many ways that can help library in its mission of "Green". Parent body of the library should also support the library in this movement.

Conclusion

In conclusion, libraries need to be greener in terms of collection development and design of their buildings. Libraries would do well to showcase their own green progress regularly, probably through starting a blog to spread awareness about green activities. All these efforts would definitely produce better green momentum in libraries and achieve a more socially responsible global profession and professionals—Greener libraries and librarians.

References

Antonelli, Monika. "The Green Library Movement: A Overview of Green Library Literature and Actions Form 1979 To The Future of Green Libraries". *Electronic Green Journal* 1, 2008: 1-11.

Aulisio, George J. "Green Libraries Are More than Just Buildings." *Electronic Green Journal* 1, 2013: 1-8.

Brown, Bill. "The New Green Standard." *Library Journal* 128, 15 December 2003: 61-64.

Connell, Virginia. "Greening the Library: Collection Development Discussion." Endnote: *The Journal of New Members Round Table* 1, May 2010: 1-15.

Divya, P.I. and Vijayakumar, K.P. "Green Libraries For Sustainable Development: New Information Technology Interfaces In libraries and Information Centers." KLA National Seminar Souvenir, July 2013: 67.

Eagan, Ann. "Noise In The Library: Effects and Control." *Wilson Library Bulletin* 65, February 1991: 44-47.

Eastman, Cynthia and Bobbi. "*Weaver. Breaking Rules Building Green Bridges* [Electronic version]." *Information Outlook*. 12 April 2008: 24-30.

Edwards, Bonnie. "Library's Community Garden to Receive Grant [Electronic version]." Goldsboro News-Argus. 27 February 2008.

Fialkoff, Francine. "Green Libraries are Local [Electronic version]." *Library Journal.* 15 June 2008.

http://www.ala.org.

http://www.usgbc.org/leed.

https://igbc.in/igbc/redirectHtml.htm?redVal=showGreenExistingBuildingsnosign.

https://www.newworldencyclopedia.org/entry/Green_library.

James LeRue and Susan LeRue. "The Green Librarian." *The Wilson Library Bulletin* 65, Feb. 1991: 27-33.

Kumar, P. Suresh. "*Greening the Library for Sustainable Development.*" 10 May, 2015<www.liscom.org/.../S%203%20Greening%20the%20Library%20for%20s>.

Larue, James. "Libraries and The Environment." *The Wilson Library Bulletin* 65 Feb. 1991: 26-43.

Loder, Michael Wescott. "Libraries With A Future: How Are Academic *Library Usage* and Green Demands Changing Building Designs?" College & Research Libraries 71 July, 2010: 348-60.

Neale, Jane. "Go Green." *Library Journal* 133, 1 February 2008: 46.

Pinkowski, Jennifer. "Keeping Track of Green Libraries." *Library Journal* 132, 15 September 2007: 27.

Sahavirta, Harri . "Showing The Green Way: Advocating Green Values And Image *In A Finnish Public Library.*" *IFLA Journal* 38, October 2012: 239-42.

Schaper, Louise Levy. "Public Input Yields Greener Library Design." *Library Journal* 128, 15 December 2003: 62.

Tomorrow's Green Library, Presented by: Andrew Logan, Emily Braithwaite, Lisa Binks, Lisa Hogarth and Stephanie Wilson.

Trotter, Dorthy Waterfill. "Going For The Green." American Libraries 39 April 2008: 40-43.